WHAT HAPPENS WHEN WOMEN PRAY

Evelyn Christenson
with Viola Blake

Scripture Press Foundation (UK) Ltd.
Amersham, Bucks.

© Scripture Press Foundations (UK) Ltd
First published in the USA 1975 by
Victor Books a division of
SP Publications, Inc., Wheaton, Illinois, USA
First British edition 1983.

ISBN 0 946515 00 X

Most of the quotations in this book are from the
New International Version of the Bible (Anglicized edition)
© UK 1979 by New York International Bible Society.
Published by Hodder & Stoughton Ltd.
Used by permission.

Other quotations from *The Living Bible* © Tyndale House
Publishers 1971.

Design and Production:
Nuprint Services Ltd, Harpenden, Herts.
Production Consultant: Rodney Shepherd.
Anglicized by Michael Perry.
Printed and Bound by Purnell and Sons
(Book Production) Ltd, Paulton, Bristol. Member of BPCC plc.

Scripture Press Foundation (UK) Ltd
Chiltern Avenue, Amersham-on-the-Hill, Bucks.

WHAT HAPPENS
WHEN WOMEN PRAY

Contents

While this book is designed for the reader's personal use and profit, it is also intended for group study. A leader's guide is available from your local bookshop or from the publisher at £2.35. Cassette recordings of an actual Evelyn Christenson prayer course based on this book, is also available at £6.50 post free (3 tapes) from the publisher.

Introduction

In 1968 I was the U.S.A. national women's chairman for the Baptist General Conference's involvement in the Crusade of the Americas. My task was to lead the women of my own church, Temple Baptist, in Rockford, Illinois to discover through six months of experimentation 'What Happens When Women Pray.' Such exciting and life-changing results were experienced from the actual praying and the methods of prayer we worked out that I began sharing them at conferences, workshops, church meetings, and conferences from coast to coast and in Canada.

In January 1972 after moving to St Paul, Minnesota, where my husband had joined the staff of Bethel College, I began six-week, and later five-week prayer courses in this area. Since then we have added one-day conferences for which the material is consolidated and presented in three sessions of about two hours each.

A committee made up of representatives from most of the churches of a given geographic area organizes and sponsors the courses. Many times participants from over one hundred different churches both Protestant and Catholic have attended.

Early in 1974 we opened the courses to men and

young people in addition to women. This has proved worthwhile as whole families have learned to pray together. Ministers take the material back to their churches to be used in prayer meetings, prayer weeks, and Bible study groups. The results are exciting.

Rev. James Jehnberg describes what happened in his church in Thousand Oaks, California as follows:

> Our Church had called in representatives of two fund-raising organizations for we needed to raise $226,000 to build an addition to our church. After listening to both presentations, and tentatively deciding which procedure to use, I asked for fifteen minutes. I quickly briefed my colleagues on your 6S method of short, simple prayers. I reminded them that, according to Psalm 66:18, if we cherish evil in our hearts, God will not hear us. Giving them specific instructions to pray confessing the sins in their lives before asking for God's guidance as to how to raise money, I divided them into six small groups and sent them off to pray in different rooms of the house. After just fifteen minutes of praying they came back together and unanimously voted what God had told each of them separately: *Don't use a fund-raising company. Borrow the money from the members of your own church.* Immediately we raised not $226,000 but $250,000 – over and above what we needed – without even going to the local bank!

After hearing the methods of prayer we developed, someone invariably asks, 'Is this material in print?'

My answer has always been the same: 'I have committed this completely to God. If He wants this in a book, He will open the doors.' Then, enlisting their prayer support, I would ask them to pray specifically, *if it were God's will,* that He would open doors. So people across the United States and Canada have prayed about this book since 1968.

The preparation of the material has been a series of

answers from God – from the taping of the courses, to the transcribing of the tapes, to the writing of the manuscript. God has placed on the heart of Viola Blake the conviction that it was His will for her to assist in the writing of the book.

Every step of the prayer course and every step in the preparation of this book has been prayed through by my Advisory Committee and telephone prayer-chains, with explicit instructions to pray *only for God's will.* We did not plan, or make contacts or 'phone calls – we only prayed.

Since we have no way of knowing who you are or what your needs may be as you read this book, our Advisory Committee and prayer-chains are continuing to pray daily that God will show you the next step in prayer that is *His will for you.*

Evelyn Christenson

CHAPTER ONE

The power of prayer

'The prayer of a righteous person is powerful and effective.' James 5:16

'Lord, help! How do I motivate eight grousers?' Here they were, on a cold Janury morning, sitting around my dining room table – the favoured ones, those who had been chosen to learn to pray. I thought they would be enthusiastic about the idea. Weren't they all leaders of women's meetings at church? Instead they sat there moaning.

Earlier, in the autumn of 1967, the national committee of our denomination had asked me to do a project for the Crusade of the Americas. 'Working with women in your own church, would you discover in a six-month period what happens when women pray?'

I had replied, 'I'll take that little task.'

It had sounded so simple in 1967. But on New Year's morning I awakened with a jolt: 'It's 1968, and I have to find out what happens when women pray!' I didn't have a single thought in my head. I didn't know how to start. I didn't know with whom I should start. What would you have done? I panicked.

But as I was lying there I said, 'Lord, please help. I

feel negative. Everything is black. It's dark and it's cold and it's everything it shouldn't be. What shall I do? Show me.'

Suddenly, just as if a door had opened over my head, God was speaking to me, though there was no audible voice. He said, 'Evelyn, if you're going to find out what happens when women pray, you are going to have to learn to use this door, the door of access to Me. This is the door of prayer. You, Evelyn, are going to have to learn to use if more effectively.'

I simply said, 'Thank you, Lord. Now I know just what to do.'

That week I called together those eight leaders of the women's meetings in the church where my husband was minister. I thought, 'This will really do it. These women will all be excited about learning to pray; they will be the committee.'

Instead they complained. 'I'm the devotional secretary of my group,' one said, 'but all the leader lets me do is close in prayer.'

Another remarked, 'My leader lets me say grace, and that's it.'

They went on and on. Evidently they didn't know what I was talking about. That's when I silently cried to the Lord for help. He answered, 'Evelyn, start from the beginning and tell them about yourself.'

'You know,' I began, 'I want to tell you something about your minister's wife. I never talk at day School, never lead home Bible study, never speak anywhere without calling on my two strong prayer partners. The three of us pray earnestly that God will enable me to speak.'

'Not you,' they said. 'not our minister's wife. You don't have any needs.'

'Your minister's wife needs prayer,' I insisted; 'she

knows very well that she can fall flat on her face if there isn't prayer support.'

I still wasn't getting through to these eight women. I had to back up some more. 'In 1961, six months after I had major surgery, I was scheduled to speak at just one session of a conference. I thought that after six months I'd be flying high, but I wasn't. A series of infections had slowed my recovery. From that standpoint, to accept the engagement was a foolish thing for me to do, but after making me comfortable in the car, my husband drove me to the conference.

'All during the evening meal I didn't say a word. I knew that if I talked then I wouldn't have enough strength to address the ladies afterward. By 10 pm. I still hadn't been called on to speak (you know how women's meetings go on and on). Weak and trembling I searched out the chairman and said, "Joyce, forget the whole thing. I don't have enough strength left to speak. I can't say one word."

'Joyce replied, "Just a minute, Evelyn." She went to summon a very mature "pray-er" whom she knew. The three of us found a little room with bunks in it, and we got down on our knees. Those two women prayed until I had enough strength to go out there and speak. At the end of the meeting we had an informal service of re-dedication, and only ten of the four hundred women present did not re-dedicate their lives to Christ.'

I had at last convinced my eight women that their minister's wife depended one hundred per cent on prayer when she went out to speak for Christ. Slowly, they began to pray.

'Oh, Lord, show me.'

'Lord, cleanse me.'

'Lord, use me.' That was all they prayed that first time, but it was a beginning.

Conversion at a country club!

Gradually, as they learned simple methods of praying effectively, God began to encourage these formerly despondent Christians with beautiful answers to prayer. The first exciting result was a dramatic conversion. I had been teaching a local weekly Bible study specifically designed to introduce women to Christ, but nothing was happening. I said to the eight women, who were now praying every Tuesday morning, 'I have a problem. Let's concentrate on one person in that Bible study group. I know that Marion doesn't know Christ as her own saviour.' That morning we prayed, and we prayed.

Then I told them, 'I'm taking Marion to lunch.' Straight away they volunteered to pray while we were at lunch, and through the afternoon. As they were leaving, one said, 'I'm going to pray that you take her to a place where you can really talk.'

Each woman took a similar specific prayer request home with her, and I drove on to Marion's house. When I got there she said, 'Let me drive.' So with my little Bible under my arm I got into her big white Cadillac convertible and we drove to her country club. Have you ever led anyone to the Lord in such a place? I hadn't, and I wasn't at all sure what was going to happen next.

Knowing that Marion's husband owned much of the shares in that country club, the host 'bowed and scraped' and asked, 'Wouldn't you like this nice secluded table here in the corner?' It was just the right spot for conversation. We talked and talked while the waitress kept bringing us coffee. I finally said, 'You know, Marion, I think it's time we stop talking and go out to the car and pray.'

What had we been talking about all afternoon?

Marion had been picking my brains about Jesus. 'How do you accept Jesus into your life?' 'What is it like to have Jesus in your heart?' 'What's it like living with Him?' So many questions! But at twenty past three Marion jumped up from her chair and together we went out to the car park, sat in that big white Cadillac, and Marion bowed her head and prayed, 'O God, forgive all my sins; and Jesus, please come in to be my Saviour.' Marion had found Christ.

Another exciting part of this story unfolded on the following Thursday morning when the dear coloured woman who helped me clean once a week opened my front door with the immediate question, 'What happened on Tuesday?'

'Why, Mary, what do you mean, "What happened on Tuesday?"'

She explained, 'Well, the Lord said on Sunday, "Now, Mary, you fast and pray," so I didn't eat; I just prayed from Sunday until Tuesday afternoon. Then in the middle of the afternoon the Lord said to me, "Mary, you can eat now." What happened on Tuesday afternoon?'

I said, 'Mary, would you believe that at 3.20 pm on Tuesday, Marion accepted Christ?'

Mary was a big person, and she put those broad arms around me, and I put my arms almost around Mary, and we stood there and cried, for she and I had prayed together for Marion by name for many months.

Prayers, not plans or programmes

We learned that things could happen when we didn't plan at all but just prayed. A long distance call came to our church after one of the Sunday morning services. It was Arthur Blessit calling from California. 'May I use your church building for a meeting on Tuesday night?' he asked. 'You won't have to do a thing. I just want to reach some hippies for Christ.'

My husband said, 'Fine, you can use our church.'

Arthur arrived on Tuesday morning. There had been no time to advertise the meeting in local newspapers or in other churches. The only means of communication had been the hippie 'underground' method. But Tuesday morning was our prayer-time. The entire kitchen area of the church was 'wall to wall' with women who had only one prayer – that somehow the hippies of the area would hear there was to be a meeting for them in our church that night.

As we were praying, our church secretary, Carolyn, came flying downstairs and interrupted our prayer with, 'The religious editor of the newspaper came to interview Arthur Blessit; now they're on their knees praying!' The religious editor received Christ. Arthur Blessit's meeting had front-page coverage that evening. How else would you get newspaper advertising in such a short time?

We had 1,100 hippies in our church that night. They had come from as far away as Chicago — ninety miles – by thumb, by motorcycle, by car. Some were on hard drugs. These characters, and I mean characters, came en masse to the service. When Arthur gave the invitation that night over one hundred of them accepted Christ. As the Christians came forward to find a place to pray with these young people, there wasn't a vestibule, or a hall-way, or a side room anywhere in the church where people weren't already praying!

My husband is a very organized man. In fact, he is now teaching a college course in management. But the next Sunday he laid aside his already prepared sermon and announced, 'I can only speak on one subject this morning: "What happens when you don't plan, but you just pray!"'

Pray first, plan afterwards

God expects us to be orderly. He expects us to manage our time, to discipline ourselves, to prepare well-planned programmes, but if we could learn to pray first and plan afterward how different would be our homes, our churches, our Christian women's clubs, our Bible studies, whatever we are doing for Christ. Maybe, just maybe, we are planning in one direction and God's will is in another direction. God might say, 'Hold everything! Turn around and go this way. This is my will for you, not that way.'

Even if we are tuned in to God's will and know we're going in the right direction, we may be going at snail's pace. God says, 'Look, you see only a tenth of what I plan for you. There are nine-tenths that you're not seeing, that you don't know anything about.'

God wants us to make ourselves available to Him, and to say before we start to plan, 'Lord, tell me what you want me to do, where you want me to go, how you want me to do it.' Then our omnipotent God, with all the abundance of heaven at His disposal, will pour out His power upon us. Instead of following our tiny, tiny plans, God wants to open heaven and flood us. It's exciting.

In our early days of learning to pray, the best source of prayer requests was the Sunday School department of our church. Gail, our children's worker, came up with a fantastic idea after she witnessed some miraculous answers to prayer. Her suggestion, 'Let's pray first and plan afterwards,' became the slogan for our church. During the children's holiday Bible club that year we set up a prayer room and collected requests along with attendance sheets. Then teachers and helpers spent their break times in prayer.

An urgent request came from one group. Not one child had received Christ though the club had been meeting for a week and a half. That Wednesday morning we homed in on that request. The same teacher was giving the same kind of Bible story, but what a difference prayer made. I stepped into the department to see twenty three hands raised to receive Christ. The spiritual ceiling of our church went straight up!

Tears of joy

The original notes I made for my report at our national conference in 1968 reveal what happened in six months as we were learning to pray:

January – the grouse session, 'Cleanse me.' 'Use me.' 'Forgive me.' 'Show me.' That was all.

February – eagerness had replaced complaining. They were excited. They were actually seeing the worth of themselves in prayer.

March – great joy and much sharing of answered prayer. They were talking about changes in their own lives due to praying.

April – there were tears of joy as we learned by experience what effectual, fervent prayer really is.

May – we were claiming victory over Satan as our specific prayers were answered in specific ways. We were learning that Satan gets busy when we actually pray, not when we study about prayer or even memorize Bible verses about prayer. But the exciting thing is that in prayer we gain victory over Satan.

June – by popular demand we opened our prayer meetings to all of our church women. In just six months we had learned that 'the effectual, fervent prayer' of a righteous person avails much – not plans or programs, but effectual, fervent *prayer*.

Recently, a high priest of the occult was quoted in our local newspaper. He said that the churches had given up the supernatural. They don't deal in the supernatural; they just deal in plans and programs and social action. He said that every human being is created with a supernatural vacuum and since Christians aren't doing anything in the realm of the supernatural, he feels that witchcraft is a reasonable substitute for Christianity.

Can we still have the supernatural in our churches? I think we can, for effectual, fervent prayer is capable of producing supernatural results.

The women of a 4,000-member church learned this in a whole day of prayer. A week later the wife of one of the four ministers told me, 'The most amazing thing happened when we learned to pray: the Holy Spirit just went "whoosh" through our church! I didn't tell you before, but we were just about to split. Our Sunday School was deteriorating Sunday by Sunday, and members were pulling out. When nothing else worked, we decided to try prayer. Problems were solved and walls betwen the factions started to crumble.'

I met her a year later and asked, 'How is it going in your church?'

Her answer, 'It's still going great.'

Unity in the community

The 'power and effect' of prayer was apparent, but there was more to come. One of the surprises was the terrific unity we found in communities where people learned to pray together. *Caution:* this refers to the body of Christ praying together, not just church members.

Last year I met the minister of the host church

where our first prayer day was held. He said to me, 'Eve, you know our daughter was killed in a tragic accident last month? An amazing thing happened at her funeral. There were priests and ministers and lay people from every single church in the area.' And then he added, 'This never would have happened if the women had not learned to pray together.'

Was it because they met for a series of six meetings? No. It was because they had learned the unifying dimension of prayer.

Marcella, wife of the mayor of a northern Minnesota town, had a fantastic vision of what God can do when women pray. One day she called and said, 'Evelyn, I'm concerned about our town. There are lots of Christians here, but we all go our own directions. We compete rather than work together for the cause of Christ. Could you come for a rally?'

One of the miracles at that rally was that there were representatives from every single church present. After the meeting a woman came to me and said, 'I'm chairman of the women's committee here, and I know why this rally was a success.'

'OK,' I said, 'you tell me.'

'Well, Marcella told us last May, "If Evelyn's coming for a rally, she expects you to be praying. Now get going." So we did and we have prayed in an organized fashion every other week from May to October.'

I was still shaking hands with the women when a beautiful blond girl stepped up to me and asked, 'Why am I here?'

I sort of blinked and replied, 'Don't you know why you're here.'

'No, I don't know why I'm here. I've never been in this church before, but this afternoon a very peculiar thing happened to me. All at once it was as if an irresistible force was urging me to come to this meeting tonight; I thought I'd better come. Why am I here?'

I looked at her and asked, 'Do you know Christ as your saviour?'

She replied, 'No, I don't.'

Then I asked, 'Would you like to?'

She said, 'Yes, I would like to.'

After I finished shaking hands we went downstairs and prayed together, and there she accepted Christ as her own Saviour.

Marcella envisaged something more for the Christian women of her town – a conference. Several months later the women who had begun to feel their marvellous unity in Christ came to the conference. One was the same little blond I had prayed with before. 'I now know what that irresistible force was.' she said. 'It was God's power. My husband has been a Christian for many years, and God has been calling him into full-time service, but I wasn't even a Christian. Now I'm going to be a minister's wife. My husband is going into training. What a horrible minister's wife I would have made, not even knowing Jesus as my Saviour.'

As we were leaving the meeting one woman remarked to me, 'I think we ought to call this the "red-eyed session." Just look around at all the tears and all the red eyes!' It was true. Women who formerly had crossed the street to keep from speaking to each other were now throbbing in one accord, in unity, loving each other in Christ. Something really had happened there. An irresistible force had been at work, as a result of prayer.

One day my husband walked in to our church and encountered our caretaker fairly dripping with perspiration. He was a giant of a Christian, but was gradually losing his ability to think and work effectively because of hardening of the arteries. As my husband saw him struggling with the vacuum cleaner he looked down, and there lying on the floor was the plug. The dear man had vacuumed the whole auditorium and didn't have the plug in the socket!

Isn't that what happens to many of us? We work, we pull, we struggle, and we plan until we're utterly exhausted, but we have forgotten to plug in to the source of power. And that source of power is prayer – the powerful and effective prayer' of a righteous person.

FOR YOU TO PRAY

'Dear God, teach me to plug in to your power. Amen'

CHAPTER TWO

Hindrances to prayer

'If I cherish evil in my heart, the Lord will not hear me.'
Psalm 66:18

'How's it going, "Mrs Chris"?' My very good friend, Steve, one of our church boys, always asked me that question when he came home for an occasional weekend from the Harvard Business School.

Some days I answered, 'Oh, it's going just great! We just learned this kind of prayer and look what's happening. It's going just great!'

Then, when he would come home other times and ask how things were going, I would have a different answer. 'We fell down this week! It was a mess. I don't know who suggested the method of prayer we tried this time, but it sure didn't work.'

Finally Steve, with his youthful fervour, was getting a little exasperated hearing of the struggles we were having as we were learning to pray effectively. I'll never forget the day he and I met by the piano in the front of the church. He stood there with his hands on his hips, and looking straight at me, asked, *'Mrs Chris, why does it take so long?'*

I said, 'Steve, I don't know. I wish I did. I'm sure it's

not God's fault. This is all experimental; it's trial and error for us. We're just learning. I really don't know why it's taking us so long.'

Steve is now on the committee of an international Christian organization, and last spring while he was teaching a management course in Atlanta, I sent him a message via one of our staff. I asked her to tell Steve that 'it doesn't take so long now.'

Several weeks later when Steve visited us at our cottage on the shores of Lake Michigan, he said, 'You know, when Jan gave me your message, "It doesn't take so long now," I had to scratch my head and wonder: What is Eve saying to me? Then I remembered my question back in 1968.'

As I stood cooking the breakfast eggs in the cottage kitchen that next morning, I explained to Steve how and why it didn't take so long. It went something like this…

Six weeks to learn

Our first prayer course was held in White Bear Lake, Minnesota with twenty different churches represented. It was a six-week course, and the women were practising simple, sometimes hesitant, audible praying. At the fifth session, one of the women shared with us that practitioners of the occult had been invited into a local school. Witches, with all their garb and paraphernalia, were instructing the students, including her daughter, in the ways of witchcraft. Of the two hundred and fifty women present, many had children in that school.

Fervent prayer really began then for those students and their teachers. In fact, women were praying so earnestly in their groups that I had to step up to the microphone and tell them to conclude their praying because the baby-sitters had to go home! God had given them an urgent reason for learning to pray quickly.

God also gave them answers to their prayers. A group of Christian parents went to school officials about the matter, and, as a result, Christian speakers were given equal time to expose the errors of the occult.

Something else was stirring in that first prayer course. It came from a group of women from a catholic church who sat in the second row. I could always count on them to be in the same place each week. What an inspiration they were. At the third session one of them came to me and said, 'Mrs Christenson, we want you to know that after just two weeks of praying we are already in "April praying."'

I had to scratch my head and think, 'April praying, April praying?' Oh yes, I recalled having told the group that in 1968 it had taken us from January to April to get to our 'Tears of joy' as we were experimentally learning what effectual, fervent prayer really was. I said, 'Tell me about your "April praying."'

She went on, 'After the very first session, all of us from our church went home, and we promised each other that though we couldn't meet together every single day, we would pray for our church every morning at nine o'clock. In just two weeks we are seeing fantastic things happen; we are already in "April praying."'

A couple of weeks later they brought me a copy of their church bulletin. One of the women said, 'Look what our minister has written!'

I read, 'If all these wonderful things happen to women who learn to pray, let's start praying as families.'

The minister even began to preach a series of sermons on prayer because that little group practiced what they had learned the very first week.

This is what's exciting to me about the prayer groups. There is always a nucleus of people, both men and women, from all denominations going back and turning their churches upside down.

I said to Steve, 'It took only two weeks for that group from that church to learn to pray. No, it doesn't take so long now.'

Six months, six weeks, six hours

One day a district leader of the Young Life Campaigners came to me with a question, 'Do you think you could teach our Campaigners to pray in six hours? We're planning to meet at a school hall, but there's going to be a wedding reception there at four o'clock, so we have to be out of the building by three.'

I blinked, and thought, *Six hours! Six weeks is one thing; six months is how long it took us at first; but now this group is asking for only six hours!* I said, 'I don't know if I can, but I'll try.'

We met together at nine o'clock in the morning. By eleven am those teenagers, many of whom were disenchanted with the established church, had pushed back their chairs and were kneeling on the floor in little circles fervently praying. I felt tears spring to my eyes at that sight – after only two hours.

Recently, in Fargo, North Dakota we had our first one-day course. I had to tell the ladies that I wasn't sure it would work, but we plunged in, breaking just once for mid-morning coffee. Then, following lunch we had an all-afternoon session. At the end of the day, the chairman said to me, 'Evelyn, the most exciting thing to me has been to hear this fervent prayer so soon by one hundred per cent of the people who have just learned to pray today.' How long does it take? It doesn't take so long.

Released to pray for others

I want to share with you one other six-week session
that took place way back in the autumn of 1964 when
my two prayer partners, Lorna and Signe, and I began
to pray together. Everything seemed to be going great
in our church. In four years our membership had almost
doubled, a building programme was in progress, and we
had a full schedule of activities to meet the needs of our
congregation. Yet, the three of us sensed that there was
a missing dimension. We decided to meet once a week
to pray for our church – a very noble idea, we thought.

We agreed at the start to base our praying on a verse
of Scripture (a good rule to follow), and straight away
God gave us Psalm 66:18: 'If I cherish evil in my heart,
the Lord will not hear me.'

'Lord, what do You mean?' we asked. 'We're going to
pray for our church.' But he continued to apply the
pressure gently: 'If *I* cherish evil in *my* heart, the Lord
will not hear *me*.' Wow! I, the minister's wife? Lorna
and Signe?

God didn't release us to pray for other needs until we
had cleaned up our own lives by confessing *our* sins. It
took us, oh, so long. We prayed and prayed, and God
kept bringing sins and sins to our minds. As our first
prayer meeting came to a close, we thought, *Phew! We
got that one over with; next week we can start praying
for the needs of the church.'* But when we met the
following week, we still couldn't get beyond Psalm
66:18! This was a new concept to us. God kept bringing
our wrong priorities, thoughts, reactions, and attitudes
to our minds. It took the three of us six weeks – six
whole weeks – to get out of Psalm 66:18 and into
effectual, fervent praying. I see one of those prayer
partners occasionally, and we still shake our heads at

the memory of it!

You don't have that many things to be cleaned up in your life…do you? Well I did, as a minister's wife. The other day someone asked me, 'What kinds of sins do minister's wives commit, or is that too personal?'

Not knowing how to answer her off the cuff, I decided to compile a list, from memory, of the many sins we confessed then. Two days later Signe stopped in the Twin Cities en route back to her home from California. 'Sig, what specific sins do you remember from those six weeks of Psalm 66:18 back in 1964?' I asked.

'The main one I remember,' she replied immediately, 'was our superior attitude concerning our spiritual status as compared to others and the idea that we should pray *for* them. God showed us that attitude was sin.' (I added that one to the two-page list I had jotted down in answer to the question!)

What other sins had we confessed?

Divided motives. All of us were very involved in serving Christ, thinking our reasons were all for His glory. But God showed us how much there was of ego, self-fulfilment, self-satisfaction, and desire to build up our own standing in the eyes of our fellow church members.

Pretence. One said it was the first time in her life she was really honest before God. People had her on a spiritual pedestal; and she didn't dare admit, even to her family, that she wasn't as spiritual as everybody told her she was. Then she confessed to God a bad attitude toward one member of her family that no one could have dreamed was there.

Pride. How surprised I was when God exposed as sin the feeling of 'look what I've done' that would come over me as I passed the duplicated copies of *my* lesson outline to the members of my Bible class. I was never satisfied in the preparation of my lesson until I had exhausted the resources in my husband's library, put the volumes of notes in outline form, typed stencils, and run off copies for all.

No, none of us had been practising any of the 'dirty dozen' sins, but God exposed one by one the 'little Christian sins' that Peter could have been referring to when he wrote,

> 'For the eyes of the Lord are on the righteous, and his ears are attentive to their prayers; but the face of the Lord is against those who do evil' (1 Pet 3:12).

A prerequisite to answered prayer

The three of us learned in a very practical way that there are prerequisites to effective intercessory prayer. There is one word we didn't touch on in the first chapter when we cited: 'The prayer of a righteous person is powerful and effective.' Did you catch what we missed? 'The prayer' of what kind of person? A *righteous* person. It is his prayer, and only his, that is powerful and effective.

If we are living in sin and liking it, if we are keeping it there, finding that it feels good, if we're nurturing, patting that little sin along – God does not hear us.

The prophet Isaiah gives a powerful description of someone in this plight. 'Listen now! The Lord isn't too weak to save you. And He isn't getting deaf' He can hear you when you call! But the trouble is that your sins have cut you off from God. Because of sin He has turned His face away from you and will not listen any more' (Isa 59:1–2, LB).

Do you wonder why your prayers aren't answered? We're going to learn many reasons why they are not in the chapters that follow, but here is the first one: sin (or sins) in your life. It is 'the prayer of a *righteous* person that is powerful and effective.' If your prayers aren't very effective, this may be the reason. Maybe it isn't. Maybe you're long past this. But I find that when I think I'm past this one, all at once some little pride pops up, and I have to confess to it quickly, get it out, and then go on.

Your problem may not be *sins*, but *sin*. And this is a very important point. When our Lord was talking to His disciples just before His crucifixion. He told them that He was going to send the Comforter, the Holy Spirit, who would convict *the world* (those who were not Christ's followers) 'of sin, because they do not believe in me' (John 16:9). This is the sin that will keep God from hearing intercessory prayer – the sin of not believing in Christ as your personal saviour. If this is your sin, the only prayer from you that God promises to hear is one of repentance and faith as you invite Christ into your life.

After we become Christians we commit sins. What do we do with them? Do we live with them? The answer is that we get rid of them. God gives Christians the formula through John, 'If *we* confess our sins, He is faithful and just and will forgive us *our sins*, and will purify us from all unrighteousness' (1 John 1:9). This is written to Christians, and tells us how we may be cleansed and ready for an effective intercessory prayer-life.

Even little sins can interfere with our communication system. We try to get through to God and there's something in the way. It may be an attitude, a spoken word. God wants these things cleared up. He doesn't want anything between Him and us. If there is, it's our fault, not His, when His ears are closed to our prayers.

Back in 1968, one dear woman objected to this. She said, 'I don't like this one bit, this cleaning up of my life before I can be strong and powerful in intercessory prayer.'

Another said, 'Not me. I have pre-school twin boys, and no matter how much I clean up my life before I start for this prayer meeting, by the time I reach here with them in the car, there's some attitude I have to get cleaned up before I can pray for others.'

I found out later that the one who objected so strenuously was harbouring a grave sin in her life. She didn't like this process, but it's very definite in God's word. This, then, is the first prerequisite – nothing between God and ourselves when we approach intercessory prayer.

How long does it take? It really doesn't take so long.

FOR YOU TO PRAY

'Dear Father, bring to my mind that sin or sins keeping you from hearing my intercessory prayers.

'I confess whatever you have brought to my mind as sin.

'Thank you, Lord, for cleansing me as you promised in 1 John 1:9 and qualifying me for effective, intercessory prayer.'

CHAPTER THREE

Praying in one accord

'These all continued with one accord in prayer and supplication, with the women, and Mary the mother of Jesus, and with His brethren.' Acts 1:4 (AV)

'Eve, this is a completely different church from what it was when we left. Why?'

To the returned missionary who asked this question, I replied, 'The answer is simple. We have learned to pray in the four years that you and your husband have been in Ethiopia.' Then I went on and shared with her how it all started in 1968, the experimentation with prayer techniques, and the method we finally came up with in those days – the small group method of prayer which we call 'Praying in One Accord.' We found this in God's Word, in the Book of Acts:

After he said this, he was taken up before their very eyes, and a cloud hid him from their sight...Then they returned to Jerusalem from the hill called the Mount of Olives, a Sabbath day's walk from the city. When they arrived, they went upstairs to the room where they were staying. Those present were Peter, John, James and Andrew: Philip and Thomas, Bartholomew and Matthew; James son of Alphaeus and Simon the Zealot, and Judas son of James.

They all joined together constantly in prayer, along with the women and Mary the Mother of Jesus, and his brothers (Acts 1:9, 12–14).

It was a new and exciting experience for us to discover that women were included at this significant time, in the life of the early church. Among them was Mary, the mother of Jesus. In this final reference to her in the New Testament, she is on her face before God, praying with the disciples, the brethren, and the other women. Wouldn't you like to have been with them in that upper room? What do you suppose they were praying about? We can't answer that question, but we do know that their hearts were throbbing together as they were praying in one accord.

Jesus, their Lord, had just left this earth. He had gone from their sight, yet the one hundred and twenty gathered in the upper room had the privilege of sensing His presence in their midst. Only a short while before, he had told his disciples,

For where two or three come together in My name, there I am with them (Matt 18:20).

Jesus was speaking of those who gather together *in His name*, not of just any group of people who meet together on earth. It is only to his followers that he gives the promise of his presence. Small group praying, the method of praying in one accord, is based on the eligibility to pray in the name of Jesus, it pertains only to the followers of Christ.

Lord, teach us to pray

We can learn something else from those who prayed in the upper room. They were putting into practice what

Jesus had taught them about prayer when he was on earth. His disciples must have felt a tremendous lack in their own lives as they saw the beautiful example of the prayer life of their Lord. In their need they cried, 'Lord, teach us to pray' (Luke 11:1).

Today, earnest followers of the Lord sense their need just as the disciples did. It's amazing that we can knock on doors, get on the telephone, invite people to our prayer groups, only to find that when we meet together we do not know how to pray. I was one of the eleven leaders who formed 5,000 prayer groups for a Billy Graham Crusade held in our area. Later, I will describe how I got involved in that. In any case, we heard afterward that fantastic things had happened in some of those prayer groups, where women had prayed for five consecutive weeks before and during the crusade. But hundreds of women have said to me, 'We did everything you told us to do. We knocked on doors, we called our neighbours. We did all these things, but we didn't know what to do when we got together. We didn't know how to pray.'

Jesus' response to his disciples and to us is simple, yet so beautiful: 'When you pray, say, "Our Father in heaven...."' You recognize that don't you? It's the beginning of what we sometimes call 'The Lord's Prayer.' What is prayer? *Prayer, real prayer, is simply conversation with God, our Father.* Jesus didn't say 'Now, when you pray, say, "My Father."' No, he used the plural, 'Our Father.' He is your Father, my Father, Jesus' Father – 'Our Father, in heaven.' It's so simple. Just conversation with God.

Changes

When people start praying together on this basis – in one accord, to our Father in heaven, in the name of Jesus – and practise praying together, things begin to change. Our lives change, our families change, our churches change, our communities change. Changes take place not when we study prayer, not when we talk about it, not even when we memorise beautiful Scripture verses on prayer; it is when *we actually pray* that things begin to happen. And we don't suffer from the 'paralysis of analysis.' We are not paralysed by analysing prayer, but we take the problems at hand and pray about them.

A newspaper reporter recently asked me in an interview, 'Would you mind telling me how much you charge for these prayer classes?'

I replied, 'We don't charge anything.'

'Well, then, will you tell me why you do it? If you don't charge what is your reason for spending all this time and effort?'

I had to stop and think a minute. Then I said, 'The reason I teach people to pray is that I have seen so many changed lives as a result of prayer. This is what makes it so exciting. We learn, not *about* prayer, but to *pray,* to converse with our Father in heaven.'

One day I received an invitation from the women of another church in our home town, to come over and teach them to pray. I said I would. A few days later, as we drove along the main road in her little red Volkswagen, the woman who picked me up took her eyes off the road and looking straight at me asked, 'Do you mind if our minister comes this afternoon?'

I was quiet for a minute because I have a 'thing' about this. I thought, 'Who am I to be teaching ministers?'

Noticing my hesitancy, she went on to assure me, 'He really wants to come.'

I said, 'OK, if he really wants to come, you tell him it's all right.' So the minister sat way back in one corner of the room while the women of his church, many of whom had never prayed out loud before, learned our six little S's of prayer. Afterward we broke into smaller groups, and I know that one hundred per cent of those women prayed that day.

A week later at a Bible class meal, I was sitting one place away from the speaker, who was the assistant minister of that same church. During the meal he leaned over and loudly asked me, 'Do you know you turned our church upside down?'

I said, 'What happened?'

He replied, 'Well, ever since our minister heard the women praying, and learned how all this prayer works, he won't let us have a single meeting unless we pray. We can't even have a book review in our church unless we pray about it!' He didn't seem too happy about the whole thing.

'I didn't turn your church upside down,' I replied. 'But it's very possible that God did.'

Recently a minister greeted me at the door when I arrived to speak to the women of his church. 'I'm so glad finally to see what you look like. A woman is here today who attended the prayer course in downtown Minneapolis. She bought a set of your tapes, and has been a little missionary circulating them among the women's circles for the last eleven months. Each circle has had its own mini-prayer group, with the women learning to pray. I can see such a difference in their lives.'

Not for women only

One night in the autumn of 1969 my husband bounced in from a church committee meeting with a message for me: 'Will you please ask the women if they will take our annual Week of Prayer the first week in January?'

Right away I shot back the answer. I didn't stop to pray. I didn't ask God what he thought about it at all. I just said to Chris, 'You tell your church committee, "No." God has called me to teach women.' But I wasn't really being honest with God.

My husband trotted back to the committee and told them, 'No, there's no way they're going to teach the whole church how to pray.'

The committee said, 'You go back to your wife and tell her that we have been watching, and we feel that the women have discovered a method of prayer that works, and we would like them to teach it to the whole church.'

By this time my husband was becoming like a ping-pong ball being hit back and forth between two bats – the church committee and me. When Chris returned with the same request, I realized that I had been hasty in my reply the first time.

I said, 'OK, I'll take the request to the women.'

Their response was also negative.

Again I agreed, but suggested that at this point we pray about it. After fervent prayer we concluded that this request was really God's way of speaking to us. We consented to take the Week of Prayer for 1970 on one condition – that it would be held in the second week in January, the first being preparation week. The committee agreed. That first week we trained prayer-group leaders from every department of the church – the choir, committee trustees and the Sunday School. They came to learn the ground rules for effective prayer.

In the week of prayer that followed, we discovered that we had about fives times as many people participating as we ever had in the past. There were boys and girls, men and women – young and old – from every area of our church life, all learning to *pray in one accord*. I don't know of one person who didn't pray, but I'll stay on the side of caution and say that of all those who attended, ninety five per cent actively participated in verbal prayer. Now, that's a lot of people praying, and there were some very definite answers that gave us great encouragement.

I recall, particularly, how thrilled the junior young people were after I had taught them our method of praying in one accord on the Sunday morning during Prayer Week. They came up with two urgent needs along with their other prayer requests: 'We need a leader and a pianist.' That morning they divided into small groups and prayed specifically that God would send them these workers. I cringed a little inside. What if God didn't answer their prayer?

On the following Wednesday, one of the church's businessmen came to Gail, our children's worker, and said, 'The Lord has laid it on my heart to be leader of the junior young people, and my wife would like to play the piano for them if she can be replaced in her present department.'

Meanwhile God had been working in the college-age class also. On the same Sunday of Prayer Week, along with specific prayer, they were offering themselves to God for service in the church. A student nurse wrote on her card, 'I am available to play the piano where I'm needed.' Gail assigned the student nurse to replace the wife in the other department, and the following Sunday the juniors almost exploded with excitement as they were presented their new leader and pianist. God had really answered their prayers!

Praying in one accord

We, as women of the church, had simply shared the method that God had given to us from the Bible, the method of praying in one accord in small groups. How is this achieved? *Simply by praying about only one subject at a time with one person praying aloud while the others in the group are praying silently on the same subject.* In this way everyone is praying together (in one accord) instead of planning other prayers in advance.

Have you ever been in a group when someone is praying a long prayer? And have you found that you were not really praying along with that person? Instead you were mulling over in your mind all the things you were going to pray about when your turn came? I have, and my thoughts have run like this, 'Lord, now bring to my mind...' 'Oh, I don't want to forget that one!' 'Say, that's a good prayer' 'Thank you, Lord, for reminding me of that one.' Then I have gone back and reviewed the prayer subjects on my fingers. Next, I've wondered what my introductory statement should be, or how I should conclude my prayer. While someone else has been praying, I have been planning my own long prayer in advance instead of praying silently on the same subject with the person who is praying audibly. That's *not* praying in one accord.

You see, if everyone in a group is praying in one accord with the person who is praying aloud, the number of prayers ascending to heaven are multiplied by the number who are praying silently. How much more power there is in prayer when the participants are really praying in one accord!

FOR YOU TO PRAY

*'Father, teach me to pray in one accord with other people, sharing **their** burdens, joys, and petitions.'*

CHAPTER FOUR

A basis for prayer – 'Six S's'

'And when you pray, do not keep on babbling like pagans, for they think they will be heard because of their many words. Do not be like them, for your Father knows what you need before you ask him.' Matthew 6:7–8

'Well, I suppose you all know how to pray. I won't fit into this group.' With that remark, Betty, my neighbour, joined the three of us meeting in a home on our block to pray for the coming Billy Graham Crusade. There she was, apparently wanting to take part, but scared to death to pray aloud, even with only three other women present.

There are thousands of people just like Betty. They are all over the country – in neighbourhood prayer groups, in midweek services, and in special prayer sessions – and they are not praying audibly for only one reason: *they don't know how to.*

We have found in our prayer seminars that about fifty per cent of those participating have never prayed aloud before. They come from a great variety of churches, Protestant and Catholic, but talking with God in the presence of others is a very real problem to them.

My response to my neighbour, Betty, was, 'Oh, yes,

you certainly will fit into this group. It's really not difficult. After we hear the prayer requests, we all are going to pray just one simple sentence on each one. And we did. The three of us, who had prayed for years, prayed one simple sentence following the request, and so did Betty! In fact, as we concluded that session, she had prayed four times, audibly. What happens when we put ourselves on the level of the most inexperienced at praying? Many of them hear their own voices in prayer for the first time.

The rules we applied that morning were the ones our women devised in 1968 to implement our method of praying together – praying about only one subject at a time, with one person praying aloud while the others in the group are praying silently on the same subject. There are *six S's,* six simple rules to follows, whether one is a participant or a prayer group leader, experienced or shy and untrained. These six rules serve as effective tools to help a prayer group get started, to encourage newcomers, and to motivate timid people to pray aloud. But a prayer group doesn't have to stay with these elementary rules. It's exciting to know that the participants can go on and graduate into effective, fervent, spontaneous praying.

Suppose your present prayer group is not going very well with no one wanting to join or perhaps not coming back after trying it once. Or, suppose you would like to start a prayer group in your church or in your neighbourhood. You may find that these *six S's* are just what you need to encourage one hundred per cent participation.

1. Subject by subject

The first 'S' is *Subject by subject* – praying in one accord about only one subject at a time. As one person prays out loud, the rest pray silently on the same subject, *not planning their own prayers in advance.* This assures complete concentration and fervent prayer on one request at a time. Also, in this way no one is deprived of the privilege of praying for the request before going on to another.

You may be accustomed to praying around the world, mentioning every person you know, every missionary in many different countries. And you may be tempted to pray this way as a prayer group leader. But your part is only to announce one subject for prayer at a time, then pray a short sentence prayer yourself. Sometimes it's a good idea to have a list ready and to say, 'Right now we are going to pray one simple sentence about so and so.' Then, as the leader, pray one simple sentence and wait for others to pray audibly on the same subject before going to the next request. Because the participants will have to 'shift mental gears' before going on to another subject, it's a good idea to pause between subjects. Then the group will be prepared to pray again.

As the participants learn to pray together, subject by subject, prayer gains momentum and becomes more spontaneous. When this happens, the leader may simply lead away in prayer on a subject rather than announcing it. When those in our groups become proficient in this method, their spiritual pulses will be throbbing together in such a way that each one will begin to sense the direction of the Holy Spirit when it is time to start a new subject. Everyone in the group will then have the freedom to initiate a new topic for prayer. It may take a while, but this is our goal. They won't need a leader anymore!

I remember the first time I tried this with my group in 1968. I had always come to the prayer meeting with a written list of requests at which I would peek with one eye. That day I told God I was going to hide the list and trust Him completely to bring to our minds those things He wanted us to remember in prayer. Checking the list after we finished praying, I was delighted and amazed to find that He had moved someone to pray about every single request I had written down!

When praying subject by subject, everyone is free to pray audibly in turn. But whether praying audibly or silently, all are praying together on the same subject, not planning their own prayers in advance, and multiplying the power of all the prayers that are ascending simultaneously to God's throne.

2. Short prayers

Short prayers, are the secret of the success of small group prayer. Just one, or only a few sentences from each person on each subject allows time for all to pray if they wish. No one should be forced to pray aloud, but let prayer be something spontaneous, something a person wants to do, even if it's only to hear her own voice in prayer.

As leaders we are responsible to see that the prayers are short. How are we going to do this? Superimpose our wills on our groups and say, 'Look everybody, let's pray short prayers'? No, but at first *we* will have to go back to basics and start praying just one simple sentence ourselves in order to get the shy, untrained ones to pray. We make the rest of the group more comfortable by being careful how we pray. Isn't God much more interested in the short statement of a newcomer who has never prayed audibly before than He is in an elaborate prayer uttered by someone who has had years of practice? It may be that we prayer veterans are inhibiting the shy ones. Some of us may even have an idea that God hears us for our 'many words.'

Christ had something to say about this when He was teaching His disciples to pray. He said.

> And when you pray, do not keep on babbling like pagans, for they think they will be heard because of their many words. Do not be like them, for your Father knows what you need before you ask him. (Matt 6:7–8).

Do we think we're going to be heard because we give an introduction, three points, and a conclusion to everything we pray about? God knows all we need, and all we have to do is to lay our requests before Him. Just think of all the requests that go unremembered when someone dominates the group with lengthy prayers on one, two, or even three subjects!

Now there are times when long, involved prayers are very much in order. If you are asked to *lead* in prayer at a meeting and respond by praying one simple sentence, you will probably jar the whole group! Long prayers are appropriate at the right time and in the right place, but that time is not when the shy and untrained are learning to pray.

3. Simple prayers

The third 'S' is 'Simple prayers'. Those who have never prayed before will find it possible to utter one *simple* sentence from the heart when the leaders and other participants avoid using complicated phrases and a special prayer vocabulary. When we leave our high-sounding theological expressions for when we are alone in prayer and make our short prayers simple ones, then the newcomers will feel comfortable about praying one simple, uncomplicated prayer themselves, and will be more liable to return the following week.

Though he didn't know it at the time, I learned a valuable lesson from one of our church leaders during our Week of Prayer in 1970. He was an Irishman with a beautiful accent and a rich vocabulary. Whenever he prayed aloud our hearts soared heavenward. But we had a problem. When he finished praying nobody else dared to follow him! Why, I wouldn't be caught dead praying after he had just uttered his long, beautiful prayer, couched in lofty theological phrases! I can remember even my husband hesitating a bit to close in prayer after this man had prayed so eloquently.

As we approached that 1970 Week of Prayer, I wondered what was going to happen in a group he would be leading. I soon found out, for one night he and I were leading our respective groups in areas separated only by a plastic curtain. As I presented the prayer requests to my group, I found it difficult to concentrate because I was so curious to learn what was happening on the other side of the curtain. Have you ever had your ear tuned in one direction while your voice was aimed in another?

I heard him open his prayer group with just one simple sentence. Astounded, I listened. But he didn't say another word. Soon, one by one, all the people in his group prayed their own simple sentences. Then he prayed another sentence on the next subject and stopped. Once again each one prayed. I was acquainted with everyone in his group, and I knew that many of them had never prayed aloud before; but that night every single person in his circle prayed aloud. What happens when we are willing to put ourselves temporarily on the level of those who don't know how to pray? We encourage them to pray with us.

Back in 1968 when we were practising and experimenting with all these methods, eventually a whole room in our church was filled with women praying; but Eva, a woman who lived next door, declared that she would not join the others in prayer. She said she had never prayed out loud in a group and she never would.

I knew that Eva's family had a very fine devotional life. She was a great Christian. This wasn't her problem, but praying aloud with others was. She would shake her finger at me in other meetings and say, 'Don't you ever call on me to pray; don't you ever call on me.'

I assured her that we never call on anybody to pray, but still she didn't come to our prayer meetings. As we drove up to the church, we would see the curtains part as she peered out the window, but that's as close as Eva got. Then one day, without explanation, she joined us. She came every week after that, but never prayed out loud.

When summer came round, we moved our meetings to one of the parks in town. It was at one of those park sessions that I had a distinct impression from God that Eva was going to pray that day. But as I led the group in prayer, mentioning one request after another, she didn't utter a word. Though it was past time for us to start home, I kept adding requests and waiting for her. Suddenly, Eva began to pray. She forgot all the rules she ever learned. It was like Niagara Falls breaking loose! That day Eva prayed around the world.

When we had our Week of Prayer in January 1970, one of the groups praying was made up of men, including the minister and the chairman of the church council...and Eva! Again my ear was attuned in another direction. Guess who prayed *first* in that group? Eva! She has said to me since, 'Eve, if I can do it, *anybody* can.'

4. Specific prayer requests

Specific requests listed and specific answers noted are a great encouragement to continuing and expanded prayer. Use a notebook, file or folder for this.

If groups start falling apart, and they may, or if people suddenly aren't interested, the best way to get things going again is to encourage them by showing specific answers to their specific requests. Whip out that little book in which requests and answers are recorded and point out how God has used the prayer group to change circumstances and individuals. Spend time in prayer *praising God* for His specific answers. Then watch as new life floods your prayer-group!

As the specific answers to their prayers pile up, you will begin to see the group members change as well. By keeping records, the individuals who are praying start to *see their own value in prayer,* and this is important.

Date your specific requests and date the answers. God is not controlled by time as we human beings are. He sends His answers down to earth when He knows best. Therefore, if we keep track of *time* – how long God takes to answer our prayers – we're going to learn some tremendous spiritual lessons about how God operates. As weeks and months and years come and go, we will see that His timing is always perfect.

We will also learn some *whys* when we keep track of how He answers. It may be that we are not ready for some answers. My two prayer partners and I prayed every week for two solid years before I had my first neighbourhood Bible study. I wasn't ready and God knew I wasn't. If we keep a record of the specific timing of our requests and God's answers, then we can look back and see many of the reasons for His delays and His withholdings.

God may answer our prayers not only at a time when we least expect, but He may answer in a *way* we don't expect. We will be astounded at *how* God answers prayer. He may answer in a way that is completely opposite to the way we think He should. He knows what is best for us, and He never makes a mistake.

Our women experienced this great joy in praying specifically in May 1968, when we were preparing for a mothers and daughters party. Ruth Johnson of 'Back to the Bible' programme, a 'daughter' of our church, was to be the speaker. We set aside a room for prayer and asked the women who came to the church to work (to prepare food, set tables, or decorate) to spend some time, equal time if they could, in prayer, praying specifically for Ruth Johnson. What a great moving of God there was at the party that night.

On the following Sunday, with my little notebook in hand (I always recorded the results of our prayer experiments), I said to Ruth, 'Please be very careful how you answer me because we homed in on you in prayer, and I want a very honest answer. This will be reported to our national conference in June. Will you tell me what happened, if anything did happen, on Friday night when you spoke at our party?.

Ruth drew a deep breath and tears came to her eyes. 'Eve', she said, 'the last time I was in this church it was to my mother's funeral. It all came back to me last Friday as I was on my way here. After I got to the church, I couldn't even bring myself to open the door. I kept thinking of my mother, and then I thought of my former Sunday School teachers who were going to be at the meal. You know, I used to be "naughty little Ruthie" to those teachers, and I had a feeling that they were all going to be looking at me and thinking: There's that "naughty little Ruthie" *again*. Evelyn, I could not walk through that door. But suddenly, I felt a great sense of strength and freedom. I can't explain it, but there was complete release and I walked in. It was just fantastic. My voice has gone around the world via radio for thirty years, but never in all those years have I felt such freedom and such power as I experienced when I sang and spoke last Friday night.'

Not long afterward Ruth's missionary brother came home from India. He came to me and said, 'Evie, what did you do to my sister?'

I replied, 'We didn't do anything to your sister.'

He said, 'Oh, yes you did. Since the women prayed, my sister has been a completely different person.'

Now I thought Ruth was a fantastic Christian before that time, but I learned something. It was that we don't limit our praying to the down-and-out, or to someone we think is dying or experiencing great tragedy. We also need to pray for those who are ministering, who don't appear to have any needs. What did we do? We only prayed – specifically. And God worked.

5. Silent periods

The next 'S' is Silent periods. Silent periods between prayers are a privilege and a blessing. Don't panic when there's a lull – just listen! This is an added dimension to our definition of prayer in Chapter 3. Prayer is a two-way conversation with God.

Today, silence is almost a lost art. After a few seconds pass without audible prayer, someone usually feels compelled to clear his throat, shuffle his feet, or nervously finger a song book. Somehow we think we have to talk *at* God all of the time, but there are marvellous things that God wants to say to us. He has answers to our questions, secrets He wants to share, yet we bombard Him with our 'many words.' We forget that God is on His throne in heaven just waiting to say something great to us, if we would only give Him a chance. How frustrated He must be (if God can become frustrated) when He has something so wonderful to tell you and me, and we aren't quiet long enough to listen to what He has to say.

One day I asked my son about a girl who lives near us, and he said, 'Oh, I guess she's fine, Mum, if she'd ever keep still so we could find out.'

'What do you mean?' I asked.

'Well, on the school bus that girl talks every single minute. She might be a real great girl, but she doesn't shut up long enough for us to find out.'

Has God ever said that about me? Has He ever said it about you? Have we learned to keep still long enough for God to say something to us? It is in the *silence* that our communication becomes two-way.

The first time I practiced the six 'S' method at a conference was 1969. It was evening, and as the women finished praying in their small groups of four, I asked them to go out to a point near the water. 'Just one rule,' I said, 'please don't talk while you are walking out to the point.' There had been fervent prayer in their groups, and I wanted them to keep their hearts open to God's voice.

We had planned that a singing trio would come to the point by boat and, at a given signal, sing to the women on shore. But the signal somehow failed, and they waited and waited, not knowing when to start their song. The leader on shore kept putting more wood on the fire and thinking, 'I *have* to say something.' But each time she thought it, God said, 'Keep still, Mary.' In fact, Mary told me later, 'You know very well, Evelyn, that God said, "Mary, keep quiet!"'

Twenty minutes went by with about five hundred women sitting in absolute silence at the water's edge. Now and then we could hear soft crying. Then from the boat totally obscured by the darkness, came the beautiful strains of 'Take my life and let it be, consecrated Lord to Thee.' The common theme that ran through the testimonies that night was: 'God spoke to me not so much in the songs or in the message, *but in the silence.*"

6. Small groups

Small Groups, the sixth 'S,' are usually best for newcomers, as well as for the shy or untrained. For some, it would take great courage to stand before a group of one hundred people, or even twenty-five people, and raise their voices in prayer for the first time. But in smaller groups they can gain confidence in praying audibly.

In our meetings when there are several hundred participants in one room, we divide into small groups of four or five. This is quickly accomplished by standing and having every other row turn back, each two rows of people facing each other. We then just move apart in groups of four, two from each row. How my heart thrilled at one of our prayer meetings in a large church recently when almost two hundred small groups of people in the same room lifted their voices earnestly to God.

Yesterday, when one of my original prayer partners 'phoned, we chatted about the joy and the privilege of being just two or three in a little group. 'Eve,' she recalled, 'when we started praying, just the three of us, that was the turning point in my spiritual life.'

Whatever we do, we must never underestimate the

value of a small group praying, for Christ promised that where two or three come together in my name, I am there with them. (Matt. 18:20). What an opportunity it provides to practise the presence of Christ!

Do you remember in the account of the stoning of Stephen that he lifted up his eyes and 'saw the glory of God, and Jesus standing at the right hand of God'? (Acts 7:55) The right hand of God is the place of authority and honour. Christ is still at the right hand of God today, interceding for us, but we also have His promise that He will be *with* us – where even two or three are gathered together. Now, we want to be very careful that we do not take Christ off His throne, that we do not play games with Him in prayer. He is in heaven, but His presence is in the midst of those who gather together in His name.

Christ helped the disciples and those who knew Him very intimately here on earth to understand this. Campbell Morgan in his sermon 'Re-kindled Fire,' emphasizes the importance of our Lord's vanishing and appearing after His resurrection. He explains that the disciples and His friends were learning the lesson that Christ was with them, even when they did not see Him with their physical eyes. These followers of Jesus were practising His presence even though they could not see Him. After He had vanished from their sight for the last time at His ascension, He was in their midst in the upper room, and they knew it.

FOR YOU TO PRAY

'Dear Father: please give me the privilege of being aware of the presence of Jesus, my Saviour, in a prayer group. Teach me to help others to pray. Teach me to listen to You speaking to me in the silent periods.'

CHAPTER FIVE

Praying in God's will

*'This is the assurance we have in approaching God:
that if we ask anything according to His will, He
hears us. And if we know that He hears us – whatever
we ask – we know that we have what we asked of Him.'*
1 John 5:14–15

On the morning following Lindon Karo's funeral, I
posed some searching questions to those attending our
prayer meeting. 'What do you think went wrong? Why
did this tremendous minister, only thirty-two years
old, die of cancer? Thousands of prayers were offered
for him. Forty people in his church had promised to
fast and pray one day a week for him. I don't think I
attended a meeting anywhere during that period, but
that we were all praying. Why weren't those prayers
answered? What went wrong? Why did we bury Lindon
Karo yesterday?'

When I reached this point in the meeting, a committee member (wanting to be helpful) waved her hand
from the back of the church, and said, 'Yes, Evelyn, and
Lindon Karo's mother-in-law and sister-in-law are here
with us today.'

Wow! I stopped for a second and pondered, *Do I go
on? Do I insult these people by teaching about how to*

pray in God's will? What do I do about these loved ones who buried their son-in-law and brother-in-law just yesterday? What would you have done? I felt God was telling me to go ahead and teach the lesson.

When the session was over, those two very beautiful Christian women came to me and said, 'Please don't worry about today's talk. Many months ago we as a family committed the whole matter of Lindon's illness to the Lord. We prayed, "Only Your will, God, whatever it is." We did not ask for healing only; we prayed that God's will be done in our loved one's life.'

Have you come to the place where you can pray, 'Only God's will'? Do you know that you are in absolute oneness with the will of God? Have you come to that place?

We read in 1 John 5:14–15 about a prerequisite to effective praying.

> This is the assurance we have in approaching God: that if we ask anything according to his will, he hears us. And if we know that he hears us – whatever we ask – we know that we have what we asked of him. 1 John 5:14–15

Did you catch the prerequisite? How can we have confidence in anything we ask? It is by praying *according to His will.* And what is confidence in prayer? It is knowing absolutely and assuredly that we have whatever we have asked.

'If it be Your will, Amen'

What do we mean when we use the expression 'praying in God's will'? Is it simply tacking on the end of prayer the phrase we use perhaps more frequently than any other? You know how it goes. We ask God for a whole

string of things, then we piously add, '…if it be Your
will, Lord. Amen.' Or it may be that we ask God for
something we know is not good for us. Let's say, for
example, that we ask for a crate of Mars bars! God
knows very well (and so do we) that if we ate a crate
of Mars bars we'd die of indigestion, but many times
we ask Him for something just as ridiculous and tack
on 'if it be Your will,' just to get ourselves off the
hook. This is not what it means to pray in God's will.

The praying person

The New Testament Greek tutor in a nearby college,
said to me one day, 'Evelyn, I hope that when you're
teaching all those women to pray in God's will that you
are teaching them that it is the person praying, and
not the prayer request, that changes.'

I said, 'That's the whole emphasis of our lesson on
God's will.'

Praying in God's will is not easy, yet it's very simple.
It involves a commitment of every single thing that
comes into our lives to God and His perfect will. And
it's exciting to live in complete oneness with the will of
God. It is never dull or static because it is not a one-
time, once-for-all commitment. It is something we have
to work at constantly, moment by moment.

This is expressed in a beautiful definition of the
word 'effective' as it is found in James 5:16. According
to Vine's *Expository Dictionary of New Testament
Words,* it means 'the effect produced in the praying
person, bringing him into line with the will of God.' It
is the person who changes, rather than the prayer.
Praying 'in the will of God' then means being conformed to the will of God as we pray. Wouldn't it be
great if we could always *be conformed to the will of God*

(with all known sin confessed), so that we would never pray outside the will of God? The effective prayer person, then, is one who is completely committed to God's will for answers, and not to his own will.

After our women had been praying for a few months back in 1968, my husband exclaimed one day, 'Even if God doesn't answer a single one of your prayers, what He's doing in the people who are praying will be worth it all.'

What God does in the lives of people who are praying, in bringing them in line with His will, is one of His miracles here in this world. The turning point in our prayer meetings is the session where people in prayer commit their whole lives to God's perfect will. This happened to a school teacher, who sent me this note recently:

> On February 26 my sister invited me to attend your prayer meeting. I thought, *A prayer meeting? What good will it do? I have prayed and prayed, and it hasn't done any good.* But I went.
>
> You see, I have been a Christian all my life. I had a wonderful Christian home and brought up in an atmosphere of loving and trusting Jesus. But, suddenly, I was faced with very severe testing of my faith. My husband's building firm collapsed, leaving a large debt for which we were half responsible. Because of this, we had to sell our home and sell everything. Also, I was not well, and our little two-year-old son had just had an operation.
>
> Then, the passage that was to change my life and my prayers, 1 John 5:14–15, "and this is the assurance...." Up to that point I had not prayed for His will. I could only see what I wanted to happen.
>
> At the end of the session Evelyn asked us to stand and form our prayer groups of four. She told us to ask God for the *one* thing we wanted most from Him. I remember saying aloud in my little circle of four Christian sisters,

"Lord, I want Your perfect will for me and my family."

That was it! I was to learn later that was what was keeping my prayers from being answered. I had never asked God for His will.

Now, I felt entirely free. I felt the whole load lift, as if the responsibility to straighten up the messy things was not mine.

. Now it is nine months since that time, and I cannot begin to tell you of the peace I have in my heart. My husband's business debts are not all cleared up as yet, but God is moving. The burden is lifted. My health has improved tremendously. In fact, I got a teaching position at Bible college this autumn, a position that just seemed to come right out of heaven itself. I was not applying or seeking such a position, but was asked to join the staff. Praise God! He can "do immeasurably more than all we ask or imagine" (Eph 3:20)

On earth, as in heaven

For us to pray, 'Lord, I want Your will down here on earth,' is a tremendous prayer. Wouldn't it be fantastic if we could pray that prayer for London today? If we could by our praying get God's will done in the USA or Moscow, or in the Middle East? While there is a sense in which we can pray that God's will be done in these places, they are not within our direct sphere of influence, are they? But there is a spot on earth, a sphere of influence that belongs only to you. It has been given to you by our heavenly Father. And it's possible for you to bring about God's complete will in your sphere of influence here on earth.

The disciples whom Jesus taught to pray, 'Our Father ... Your will be done on earth as in heaven,' knew they couldn't change the whole Roman Empire, but they also knew it was possible for them to change the spheres of influence which were theirs, which had been given to them by God. And they did. God changes circumstances and people when we in a very personal way pray that His will be done in the sphere of influence which is ours.

The Lord's Prayer really comes into focus right where we are when we pray, 'Your will be done on earth as in heaven.' Is there anything contrary to God's will in heaven? No! Think of what would happen if every Christian really brought God's will to the little sphere that is his, with nothing contrary to God's perfect will! How different would be our nation, our cities, our churches, our homes.

The example of Christ

The supreme example of praying in the will of God is that of Christ praying in the garden of Gethsemane on the night before He was to die on the cross for our sins. Our Lord, in His humanity, did not want to suffer. He prayed, 'Father, if You are willing, take this cup from me; yet not my will, but Yours be done' (Luke 22:42). Then, after much agony of Spirit, He said: Father, I am willing for Your will.'

Have you come to the place in your life where you can say, 'Lord, not my will, but Yours be done? No matter how much it hurts, how difficult the task, how high the mountain You've given me to climb, it doesn't make any difference, dear Lord, I am willing'?

When we visisted the Holy Land a few years ago, I sat alone under one of those old, gnarled olive trees in the garden of Gethsemane, and read in Luke's Gospel the account of all my Jesus went through the night before He died, before He took upon Himself the sin of the world, including mine; when He sweated as it were great drops of blood there in the garden. With my heart absolutely breaking, I wrote in the margin of my Bible,

'Lord, please, only Your will in my life, only Your will!' We don't have to sit under an ancient olive tree in His land to come to that place, but right where we are today we can say to Christ, 'Lord, not my will, only Yours be done.'

When we reach the place where we're really on our faces before God, does He as an 'ogre' sitting up in heaven say, 'Good, I have another doormat on which to wipe My feet'? Is that what He says? Do we become doormats for God to wipe His feet on when we say, 'Lord, I'm willing for Your will'? Oh, no. What happened to Christ the day after He said this to His heavenly Father? He became the *Redeemer of mankind!* He became your Saviour and my Saviour.

Mary, too, had a tremendous privilege because she was willing for God's will in her life. Do you recall her response at the time of the Annunciation? When the angel came to her and said that God had chosen her to be the mother of the Saviour, Mary immediately responded, 'I am the Lord's servant. May it be to me as you have said'.

Do you think it was easy for Mary to say yes to the will of God, to being pregnant out of wedlock? When it meant vulnerability to misunderstanding, to ridicule? When it could mean possible rejection by her fiancé or even being stoned to death? It was not easy for Mary, but because she was willing for God's will, she was greatly blessed by Him. She was given the great privilege of bearing the Son who became our Redeemer.

Open doors

What happens to Evelyn when she is on her face before God and says, 'OK, Lord, I don't know what You want. That's a big mountain, that's difficult surgery, these are hard things in my life, but, Lord, no matter what it is, I want Your perfect will'? At that point does God become an ogre and take advantage of my commitment? No, at that point He starts to open doors, and fantastic things begin to happen – even prayer conferences – when I just make myself available to Him.

One day our college chaplain inquired, 'Eve, how did you ever get all those prayer meetings started, anyway?'

I shrugged, 'They just sort of grew, like Topsy.' He looked at me, wondering at what I was saying. I went on, 'You know, we really didn't plan them. They just happened. In every single step, the constant prayer of local committees, prayer chains, and our general committee has been, "Lord, Your will." Then we wait to see what His will is. We never even make contacts asking to hold a course, and it is so thrilling to watch God work when we let Him.'

One day a young woman who had travelled almost one hundred miles round trip each day to attend a Minneapolis prayer conference asked me, 'What is the procedure to get you to come to our town for a prayer conference?'

I replied, 'Pray about it, and if it is God's will, we'll come.'

'Oh, three of us have been praying for several months,' she replied, 'and we believe God is saying we should have it.'

'That's good enough for me,' I said. 'I'll come.'

I better understood her insistence on having a conference in her town when she handed me this note:

Dear Evelyn: since being in your prayer conferences my life has been changed through accepting Christ. Also, my four-year-old daughter and nine-year-old son have asked Jesus into their lives. Now my husband wants me to work on him. Thank you.

God rewarded her eagerness when thirty women found Christ in 'her' conference. It was God's will!

In fact, the inter-church Bible study on prayer, that automatically turned into our first prayer conference, came into being because God took over. The chairman and I, frustrated at not being able to work my schedule into all the autumn events of that area, finally in tears just prayed together, 'All right, Lord, only *Your* will. Whenever *You* want this Bible study, let it work out.' And God timed it perfectly. He knew all along when prayer would be needed in that town. He knew that the next February, witches and occult personnel would be in one of the high schools, so He planned for those two hundred and fifty women to be 'praying together' just at the right time.

What has turned into this whole prayer ministry in my life started in November 1967, when I was asked to work on the prayer experiment with our church women, as described in Chapter One. I hesitated at first, not knowing for certain whether to make the commitment. But one day while I was reading God's Word, a phrase in Revelation, 'See, I have placed before you an open door,' stood out as it it were in bold print. God said, 'Evelyn, I have placed before *you* an open door.' I closed my Bible, said, 'Lord, I'm willing,' and went to make a long-distance 'phone call. I said excitedly to the secretary of our National Women's committee, 'How can I say no when God has just put before me an open door in Revelation 3:8?'

Has God put before you an open door? Are you hesitating, perhaps rebelling, or holding back because of fear, when God is challenging, 'Look, here's an open door, wouldn't you like to walk through it for Me? This is My will for you.'

Oh, answer Him, 'Lord, here I am. There is no friction

between my will and Yours. Whatever You have for me,
I know that You will give me enough strength, enough
grace. I know You will give me all that I need, so Lord,
here I am ready to do Your will.'

'Try it. You'll like it!' It's amazing what happens
when we step out.

Men too?

Sometimes I seem to need a little help from other
people in going through the doors God is opening for
me. 'I don't think God is keen for you to teach men to
pray, but I think you are,' a full-time church worker
chided as we chatted at a Christmas party. I suddenly
realized that I was so sold on the idea that I was
praying, 'God, Your will,' but didn't have the courage
to accept it.

My prayer-chains had been praying for several
months about frequent requests for me to attend prayer
meetings. Then I learned that, while I was planning to
give a three-minute speech the next Sunday encour-
aging attendance at our up-coming meeting, the host
church was planning for me to give *the* morning talk. I
was panicking, just *knowing* it never could be God's
will for me to do *that!*

Suddenly, as we were together praying, a prayer-
chain member prayed, 'Lord, we're sick and tired of
praying this request. We're going to test it. The way
the men accept Evelyn next Sunday morning will be
our answer as to whether she opens the prayer meetings
to men or not.' I nearly fainted as she prayed. *I* never
would have dared talk to God like that.

The next Saturday I received a call from a woman in
one of St. Paul's suburbs. 'I've met with some of our
leaders (we're without a minister at present), and we

want an evening prayer meeting in our church that is open to men, women, and young people. We definitely feel it is God's will.'

'I'll give you my answer on Monday,' I stalled, not daring to tell her I had to see how the 'test' came out the next day!

With fear and trembling I shared 'What Happens When We Pray' with that Sunday congregation. After the service the knuckles of my right hand were white from all those men shaking hands and thanking me. Nine days later we started our first prayer meeting for women *and men*. Sometimes I need a little pushing to go through doors God is opening. Do you?

If you want me, Lord

One Friday afternoon during our first prayer meetings, I asked my small telephone prayer-chain of ten members to pray that God would keep my schedule in balance speaking against the occult and on prayer. That night, in one of those deep devotional times that come periodically in many of our lives, I prayed, 'Lord, I don't know what it is, but I want Your will, just Your will.' And I meant it. Then, out of the blue it seemed (but I'm sure it was God-inspired), I heard myself promising God that I would be involved in two areas if He wanted me to. One was the Billy Graham Crusade which was due to be held that coming summer; the other was a national women's prayer movement.

The very next morning my telephone rang. It was Myrl Glockner. She said, 'Evelyn, we've never met, but I just felt I had to call and ask you if you will be one of eleven committee members to get 5,000 prayer groups going for the Billy Graham Crusade. Do you want time to pray about it?'

I was stunned, 'Myrl,' I stammered, 'I don't need time to pray. How can I say no when just last night I said so completely, "Lord, Your will, if You want me to be involved in the Billy Graham Crusade."'

On the following Tuesday, after I had completed a session on prayer, a woman came down the aisle of the church waving a paper and calling, 'Evelyn, I have a message here for you from Vonette Bright of the Prayer Crusade. She would like you to become involved in the programme.'

Friday, Saturday, and Tuesday. There it was – God's opening of two doors when I told Him I was willing for His will for me with those two organizations. It's a very exciting thing. Don't say, 'I want it my way, Lord,' but 'Lord, Your way. Whatever You have for me, I'm Yours. Just take me, open any door, lead me in that direction.' You will be astounded at what God will do. You will be out of breath trying to keep up with the opportunities. Phone calls will come from people you didn't even know existed. Who inspired that person to call and ask you to go here or there to minister? Nobody – but God.

FOR YOU TO PRAY

'O God, I want only Your will in my life. Open the doors You have for me, and give me the courage and faith to go through them.'

CHAPTER SIX

Commitment in prayer

'So then, those who suffer according to God's will should commit themselves to their faithful Creator and continue to do good.' 1 Peter 4:19

In order to pray effectively in God's will, you may have to get a new view of God – a God who never makes a mistake. Our daughter Jan was still in secondary school when a friend of hers was in a serious accident just before Bank Holiday. Not knowing whether Rick was dead or alive, she went down to see his demolished car.

I was standing at the kitchen sink doing dishes when Jan came in trembling. Describing the car, she wondered how they ever pried Rick out of that crushed front seat. Suddenly she said, 'But, Mum, God never makes a mistake!' And turning on her heels, she rushed upstairs sobbing, and threw herself across her bed.

It was a few years later while she was still in college that Jan came home because our family was going through a crisis. Once again she stepped into that same kitchen, and after we had wept together, she backed off, raised her finger at me and said, 'Now, Mum, don't *you* forget, God makes no mistakes.'

An omniscient Father

Is your God an all-wise Father, who knows the end from the beginning, who knows all the causes and all the outcomes, and who never makes a mistake? We may pray for something that seems very good to us, but God knows the 'what ifs' in our lives. He knows the calamities that might occur if He answered our prayers in the way we think best. He also knows about all our difficult situations and wants to turn them into something tremendously good.

This view of God as an omniscient Father comes into focus very clearly as the years pass. One of the advantages of growing older is that we can look back and see that God has not made a single mistake in our lives. Maybe we'll have to get to heaven before we understand some things, but it's exciting to recognize as the years come and go that everything has worked together for good if we really loved Him. When we keep a record of what is happening to us, it isn't long before we realize that the difficult things are there for a reason, and God is making no mistakes.

Pray requests – not answers

When we first started a telephone prayer-chain in our church, I, as leader, soon learned that it was a full-time job. With sixty-six members signing up and averaging four, five, sometimes six prayer requests per day, it became more than I, as a minister's wife, had time to handle, so I turned over the leadership to another woman. When Elmy took over I said to her, 'You're going to have a problem. Some people will be calling to give you *answers* instead of requests. When they ask you to pray that such and such will happen, tell them kindly, "We do not pray answers, we pray requests."'

Do you see the difference? When we pray answers we're demanding that God do something and telling Him we want it done now – 'just the way we want it, Lord,' When we're bringing our requests to Him, we're saying, 'Lord, here's the need' (the circumstance, the person, whatever it may be); then we ask Him to answer according to His omniscient will.

Even with our motives, it's easy to pray answers rather than requests. One woman on a prayer-chain to which I belong is a returned missionary to Africa. After she and her family came back home, they all wished they were back on the field, so they started to pray, 'Lord, send us back to Africa.' They even reapplied for the position they had vacated.

One day I received a telephone call from this dear lady. She was sobbing. 'Eve, we have just heard from our headquarters that the position we held is filled, and we can't go back. Oh, Eve, we prayed and prayed that God would send us back to Africa.'

What could I say about her praying that beautiful, noble 'answer' to God? 'I tried to comfort her: 'You prayed the wrong prayer. If God had wanted you back on your mission station, He could have kept that position open till your letter arrived. It must not have been His will.'

A pawn in God's hands?

I was discussing this with someone and she said, 'Look, I'd feel like a pawn in God's hand if I ever prayed that way.'

I thought for a minute. Then I said to her, 'You know, maybe the greatest privilege in the whole world will be for me to be a pawn in the hands of God, who never makes a mistake. Just think, I'd never have to do anything by trial and error. I'd never fall down on anything (which I do very frequently). If God were in control of my every action, I would never do anything wrong. What a privilege to be a pawn in God's hands!

But God hasn't quite chosen to do things that way, has He? God has given me a free will, and He has given you a free will. He has given us the privilege of saying, 'All right, Lord, I'm free. I have a free will, but I want to do what You know is not a mistake in my life.'

I'm not being a pawn on a chessboard if I say willingly, 'Lord, I really don't know what the best approach would be, where I should go, when I should start.' With my free will I can say, 'Now, Lord, You know all the "what ifs" and all the outcomes. So, Lord, in my free will, you just use me to bring about your perfect will here.'

Are your motives right?

How can you be sure that we are not asking wrongly? James writes, 'When you ask, you do not receive, because you ask with wrong motives, that you may spend what you get on your pleasures.' (Jas 4:3). Let's never insult God by saying, 'O Lord, that other woman's husband looks just a little bit good to me. Is it OK if I just sit at his feet – in my imagination? There won't be anything physical about our relationship, Lord.' Let's not ever ask whether that can be God's will. We know what His will is, and He says, 'Be holy, for I am holy.'

Perhaps we say, 'Lord, *look* at that new car, that new house,' or 'Wow! Look at her wardrobe, Lord, look at it! Is it OK if I'm just a little bit jealous?' Now, we don't really ask God such questions, but we often rationalize our feelings and attitudes in an attempt to justify them, don't we?

It may be that we're a little bit touchy. We whimper and complain, 'Lord, she rubs me the wrong way. Look what she did. I really don't like her very much. Could that be Your will, Lord?' No. God's Word says, 'Love does not demand its own way. It is not irritable or touchy' (1 Cor 13:5, lb). So one sure way of not asking amiss is to know God's Word, the Bible. If God calls it sin, don't insult Him by asking about it.

But the Bible isn't all negative. We find in God's Word what we *can* do and what we *ought* to do. Responding to the positive commands of God's word is another prerequisite to answered prayer based on obedience: 'If you remain in me and my words remain in you, ask whatever you wish, and it will be given you.' (John 15:7). There is nothing in God's Word that is contrary to God's will, is there? If we find it in His Word, we can believe it, we can live it, and we can act upon it.

At this point you may be asking, do we dare to pray for somebody's salvation? Is it God's will? Peter tells us, 'The Lord is . . . not patient with you, not wanting anyone to perish. (2 Pet 3:9). We are to pray for those outside the body of Christ, but we must not forget that the person for whom we are praying has a free will, just as you and I have. God never superimposes His will upon anyone, but the timing and the sovereignty are His. Pray, yes. It is God's will that we pray that everyone will be saved. In answer to our prayers, the Holy Spirit moves in that person's heart, but we are to leave the results with God.

There is one more way we can be sure we don't ask wrongly. God's Word tells us we believers have two Intercessors – Christ at the right hand of God and the

Holy Spirit dwelling in us. The Holy Spirit takes our prayers when *we don't know what we ought to pray* and brings them to the Father 'in accordance with God's will' (Rom 8:26–27). At those times when we cannot even put the deep yearnings of our hearts into words, we can rest assured that the Holy Spirit is interceding for us before the throne of God according to the Father's will.

When God says no

Is it ever good when God says no? I had a negative answer when we first moved to St. Paul. I was asked to be the chairman of a large hospital committee. I knew nothing about the two hospitals they served, but was assured it was a 'you-won't-have-to-do-a-thing' job.

I immediately called back home to the prayer-chains I had just left, asking them to pray for God's will. Soon the answer came from them and from others I had asked to pray: 'God is saying no.' And He was telling me 'No' also.

When I told the committee what God had said, I almost felt the eyebrows being raised in surprise. I could not understand either why God would say no to such a great job when I was lonely with nothing to do in my new town.

A couple of weeks later, I found out why. The committee chairman was transferred with her husband out of state. Within two weeks, I would have been chairman of an organization that ran coffee shops and gift shops, and supervised volunteers and students in two large hospitals. In addition, the whole work was needing to be reorganized by the hospital administrators – a process which is being completed only now, four years later. What a mess I would have made of that gigantic job!

'O dear, God,' I prayed, 'thank You for knowing the 'what ifs' and for keeping me from making a mistake in this my new home town.'

Is suffering ever God's will?

One year in our neighbourhood Bible study we discovered a verse of Scripture which had a great impact on all of our lives. I knew the concept was scriptural, but I had never noticed it in God's Word before. 'So then, those who suffer according to God's will should commit themselves to their faithful Creator and continue to do good.' (1 Pet 4:19).

Those who suffer according to God's will – is that in the Bible? Yes, it is. And almost everyone in our group that year was suffering. Of course, they weren't suffering because they were in the Bible study group (I hope!). They were suffering in their bodies and in their spirits in various ways, but they began to see tremendous things take place. Whenever a problem or a crisis arose, God gave us a specific answer immediately, in His Word, and we received strength, grace, peace, maturity in Christ – whatever was needed.

The husband of one woman in that group had a peculiar fungus growing under his skull, and his only hope for survival was in the administration of a drug that had side effects on the mind and personality. He became an entirely different person. As a result he divorced his wife and turned his back on his whole family. Recently, I had lunch with this woman. She's still radiant in Christ.

Another member's husband had contracted syphilis and had to name all his partners, a whole string of them. That woman found strength in the Word of God.

Two unmarried daughters of one woman, both teen-agers, became pregnant, as did a teenage daughter of another woman. About the least that happened to any-body was major surgery or breast cancer!

Can suffering be God's will? Yes, we all saw it come into focus in 1 Peter. If you're suffering read that letter. It's tremendous. We, as Christians, aren't promised that we'll be free from suffering. Sometimes we suffer simply because we have frail, human bodies, but if we're commiteed to the God who doesn't ever make a mistake, we can have the assurance that He has permitted our suffering and *has a specific reason for it.*

I have no way of knowing whether you are suffering as you read this chapter, but if you are, while you are, can you truly pray, 'Lord, I still want Your will, Amen'? It means taking every facet, every area of our lives, and turning them over to the Lord. It's easy to pray, 'Lord, how I love Your will' when we're on the moun-tain-top. But there are other times when we can only pray, 'O Lord, I'm in the valley and it hurts. But, Lord, my answer is yes. I know that Your will is right, and I'm willing to conform to Your will no matter what it is.'

God works for our good

Way back in our college days, I faced a crisis when I lost my third pregnancy. I had already had a mis-carriage, then a full-term still-born, and now another miscarriage. 'Lord, Lord, why all of this?' my heart cried.

It was just after World War II, and we had returned to college after Chris had promised God in a burning bomber over Berlin that he would become a preacher after the war was over. Then God allowed us to lose this third baby. Was He turning His back and letting us suffer?

No, not at all. God gave me at that time Romans 8:28, 'And we know that God works for the good of those who love Him. I loved Him, and Chris loved Him, and God had His reasons for not allowing those three babies to live.

What all of God's reasons were, I may never know short of eternity. But one thing God seemed to tell me was, 'Do you think that you and Chris could have gone through seven more years of schooling if you had had those three babies? Your dad had become an invalid and Chris's dad had died leaving two younger children. Could you have had the courage and the financial support to face seven more years of schooling with three babies to care for?'

Did God make a mistake? No. Not at all. Romans 8:28 has been our family's life verse ever since. We know that *all* things, absolutely everything, work together for our good. This was the omniscient God who never makes a mistake dealing in the lives of those who love Him.

Despite my earlier miscarriages Jan came along normally and then, when we were in our first pastorate, it seemed God was giving us a second healthy child. But Judy lived to be only seven months old. And all the pain came back again. 'Lord, how come? Haven't I suffered enough? Haven't I learned?'

When God took Judy, He spoke to me so clearly from Hebrews chapter 12: 'Our fathers disciplined us for a little while as they thought best, but God disciplines us for our own good, that we may share in His holiness.' God said, 'Look, Evelyn, this is for your profit. If you're going to be a minister's wife, you will have to under-

stand some of these things.' I wish I could write of all
the ways that God through the years has used that
experience for my profit as I've stood with heartbroken
parents by tiny caskets or hospital cots.

Ultimately God did permit us to raise three happy,
healthy children, Jan, Nancy, and Kurt. And He had
things to teach us through each of them, as well as
through those we lost.

Do we ever arrive? My mother-in-law once said to
me, 'Oh Evelyn, I'm over seventy and I still haven't
arrived.' No, we never arrive, but God is doing something. He's making us what He wants us to be. It's in
the suffering, and it's in the hard things that He wants
us to say, 'Lord, you never make a mistake. I want only
your will.'

When I was speaking about this at an evening
meeting near my home, three young women came to
speak to me. I learned that one of them was going
blind, one had just lost her two-year-old son in an
accident, and the other was facing hip surgery within
the next few days. As they spoke to me individually,
each said that Romans 8:28 had come into focus for her
that night. And each added, 'I am now willing for God's
will, whatever it may be.'

The other half of God's will

Are you willing for God's will? In the previous chapter
I wrote about the open door and the excitement. That's
half of it, but the other half is being willing for Gods
will no matter now hard it is. At one of our church
circle meetings, our leader, whose only sister was dying
of cancer, said while leading our devotions, 'I have
struggled for months and months. Now I can finally
tell you that if God takes my sister or lets her live, I am

willing for God's will.'

Her words completely broke us. We forgot everything on the agenda and started to pray. There were women there with very serious problems. A young, pregnant mother who had lost her only other child to cot death syndrome the preceding March could say, 'I'm willing for God's will in this pregnancy.' Another lady suffering from Hodgkins disease could say the same. Each of those women prayed and meant it, 'Lord, I'm willing for Your will!' Then they immediately went to intercessory prayer for me while I spoke at the church where the minister in charge of young people later said to me, 'You turned our church upside down!' If you and I want to be powerful intercessory pray-ers, we must be willing for God's will not only in the things for which we are praying – that's only half of it. The other half is *being willing for God's will in our own individual lives.*

Hot fires

At Lindon Karo's funeral, my fourteen-year-old niece was sobbing her heart out; she loved her minister dearly. As I put my arms around her, I said, 'Carla, God must have something very, very great for you if He's giving you this hot a fire so early in life.' What did I mean? I meant that God has a way of making us greater persons by the 'hot fires' which are preparing us for what is ahead. This is a beautiful concept.

Our Jan learned this when she was in the senior school. Her friend, Dave, was a fantastic boy, president of the student's union, as well as senior student in his year. He was captain of the basketball team, and had singlehandedly pitched the local baseball team to the world championship. His poetry had been published

nationally – everything was going for him with two
exceptions: Dave was not a Christian, and he had
leukemia. But he didn't know about the leukemia and
neither did Jan.

In the spring of that year, our local churches spon-
sored a gigantic youth rally wth Dave Wilkerson as
the speaker. At first Jan was timid about inviting
Dave, but she finally worked up the courage. On the
evening of the rally, Chris and I took the car and drove
them over. My husband sat close enough to Dave to
hear him pray as he slipped to his knees at the end of
the service: 'Dear God, forgive all my sins and, Jesus,
come into my heart as my Lord and Saviour.'

Dave had no idea at that time that he was soon to
enter into battle with a deadly killer – leukemia. By the
end of term Dave knew he was very sick, but hardly
realized how near the end was. He wrote to Jan: 'Dear
Jan, Thank you for introducing me to Christ. You'll
never know what He means to me now, and what He
will in the future.'

Two weeks later, Dave's 'future with Christ' was a
reality. Early on the day he died, I was sitting alone in
my purple chair in the living room. Sensing that
something was wrong, Jan got out of bed, came downstairs and asked, 'Where's Dad?'

I said, 'He's at Dave's house, love.'

She said, 'Dave's gone, isn't he?'

I replied, 'Yes.'

For a little while we sat and cried together in that
little purple chair. I said, Jan, God is making you finer
gold.' She had heard that many times in our home. We
talked about Romans 8:28, and Job's assurance that
'When He has tested me. I shall come forth as gold' (Job
23:10). That morning I said to Jan what I recently
repeated to Carla at Lindon Karo's funeral, 'God must

have something great in mind for you to give you all
this 'fire' at your age.' Then Jan sobbed, 'Oh, Mother,
what if I hadn't invited him to hear Dave Wilkerson
preach?'

Dave's funeral was the largest that had ever been
held in our city. Hundreds of teenagers, teachers, and
school officials were present. As my husband stood up
to speak, he said, 'I can almost hear the basketball
bouncing in heaven today.'

Then he told all those people what Dave had said
just before he died. He had raised himself from his bed
and asked, 'Where am I?'

His mother had replied, 'Dave, you're in Billings
Hospital in Chicago and you're very, very sick. But all
the doctors and nurses are here.'

Then Dave had said, 'Oh, no. Where I am it's all
green and beautiful.' And then he had died.

My husband could tell all those teenagers and the
others that Dave was with his Christ in a future that
was only two weeks away when he had written about it
to Jan.

Suffering can be according to God's will. Are you
willing – even if suffering is to be a part of your future?

Committed to His will

At our session on this subject we invite participants at
prayer time to commit their lives to God's perfect will.
On a Wednesday morning, following such a session,
one woman who attended committed her whole life,
everything she held dear, to God's will. That very
weekend her husband was killed in a motorboat
accident! On the following Wednesday, one of the group
members came with a message from this widow. 'Please
tell Evelyn that God prepared me for this experience

when I committed my life to Him for His will last Wednesday.'

Several months later at a prayer leaders' workshop, with tears in her eyes, she told us that she could really see God's will in this tragedy because one of her daughters who had turned away from Christ and left home had come back to Him, and was now taking her Daddy's place in leading the smaller children in Bible reading and prayer each day.

After prayer time in a seminar the following February, a young woman whose husband was training for the ministry said to me, 'I cannot pray for God's will in my life. I cannot do it.'

When I asked why, she replied, 'I prayed and prayed and prayed for a baby. Then I became pregnant and was so excited, because I knew it was an answer to prayer, I knew God had given us that baby! But last December I had a miscarriage – and now I don't have my baby.

I said, 'God doesn't make mistakes. He gave you the child for just the few months that you carried it. God has accomplished His purpose for that baby's life.'

The young woman thought for a moment, and said, 'Now I can pray for God's will.' We bowed our heads and she prayed, 'Lord, whatever it is, I want only Your will in my life.'

Again, following a session on God's will, a young person who had undergone surgery for a brain tumor about five years previously struggled up the aisle with the help of two sticks, and asked if he could say something. We all thought he was going to ask for prayer for healing or make some other request. But, supported on either side by his 'new' mother and myself, he leaned toward the microphone and said, 'I just want to thank God for these sessions and for the privilege of being here. You know, my mother died while I was still in a coma after my accident.' (He called his brain tumor his accident.) Then he added, 'If all these things hadn't happened to me, I would not have come to live with this new mother who is a Christian. She has introduced me to Jesus, and I have received Him as my Saviour. If I hadn't had my accident, I would never have come to know Jesus.' Then he said, 'I'm willing for anything that God's will has for me.' And he stood there, not even able to support himself, but willing for God's will.

The place of praise

We may reach the place suddenly, or it may take us years to realize that God isn't making a mistake in our lives. But then we are at the point where we can praise Him. A new Christian in my Bible study called me one day and said, "'Mrs Chris,' I think I found a wrong translation in the Bible. It's there in the first chapter of James, verses two to four. Isn't it wrong when it says, 'Consider it pure joy, my brothers, whenever you face trials of many kinds.'?"

I smiled over the phone and said, 'No, it's not wrong. This is the place you reach when after years and years of trials and difficulties, you see that all has been working out for your good, and that God's will is perfect. You see that He has made no mistakes. He knew all of the possible outcomes in your life. When you finally recognize this, even *during* the trials, it's possible to have joy, deep down joy.'

And Philippians 4:6 comes into focus at this point:

'Do not be anxious about anything, but in everything, by prayer and petition, with *thanksgiving,* present your requests to God.'

It is a privilege to see God being glorified in our lives. We are to give thanks always, knowing that we have a God who never makes a mistake. And if we are going to be effective in prayers, praying in the will of God, it's not something we tack on to the end of our prayers. It's a commitment to God's will, a way of life. It's being willing for His will in the things for which we are praying and in our personal lives. And it's 'always giving thanks to God the Father for everything, in the name of our Lord Jesus Christ. (Eph 5:20). As I said earlier, it's easier said than done – but the rewards are fantastic!

FOR YOU TO DO

Bow your head, close your eyes, and **think** of the most important thing in the world to you. (It may be health, a loved one, a job, money, education, etc.)

Now pray:
   'Father, I want only Your will in this thing that is most important in the whole world to me.'

Now in prayer thank God for however He chooses to answer, knowing it is according to His perfect will.

Please don't pray the following prayer unless you really mean it.
   *'Father, I want Your will in **every area** of my life. including my job, my home, my health, my children, my loved ones, and my service for You. Amen.'*

CHAPTER SEVEN

Where to pray

*'When you pray, go into your room, close the door and
pray to your Father, who is unseen. Then your Father,
who sees what is done in secret, will reward you.'*
Matt 6:6

My old green chair has long since been reupholstered,
but years ago, when it was brand new, it became the
quiet place to which I would steal very early in the
morning to spend time alone with God. It was on my
knees at that old chair that I would pour out the inner-
most groanings of my heart – for only God to hear.
Groanings much too personal to be heard by any other.
My tears stained its cushion as I knelt interceding for a
loved one. It was there I was filled with awe and
adoration for God and all He is – 'the heaven, even to
highest heaven, cannot contain Thee' (1 Kings 8:27).
   It was there on my knees with my open Bible that
God taught me to wait on Him for every point in a
series of addresses. It was there with my head buried
in my hands that I begged God for wisdom for a certain
talk that I was to give. Not getting any answers, I
reached for the morning newspaper, laid it on the seat
of the chair, and read in the headlines that Russia had

sent Sputnik I into outer space. Then God said, 'It isn't who can *conquer* outer space that counts, but He who *created* it and in whom all things hold together' (see Col 1:16–17). I had my subject!

Private prayer – public praying

Do you have a secret place for private prayer, a certain corner, a particular chair, or a room set apart where you can spend time alone with God? A room where you daily *shut the door* to pray to your Father in secret? The group concept of prayer is important, and we do need to pray *with* one another: 'Let us not give up the habit of meeting together' (see Heb 10:25). But the going away to pray in secret is perhaps the most vital type of prayer in which we engage. It is also an indicator of the kind of prayer group participant we really are, for *it is our private praying that determines the quality and validity of our public praying.*

Though we are never to be critical of the prayers of others, we can often recognize in our prayer group those who have spent time in private prayer and the others who have come perhaps to do the only praying that they have done all week. Some struggle and strain to sound pious, but it's obvious that they haven't experienced the deeper dimension of private prayer.

Have you ever seen a bright blue iceberg? In Alaska recently I stared in awe at a mountain lake filled with beautiful blue icebergs that had broken off Portage Glacier. Immediately my mind went back to an article I had read in a family magazine that compared our secret praying to an iceberg. The 'absolutely no boating' sign reminded me that eight-ninths of the bulk of an iceberg is below the waterline – out of sight. Only one-ninth is visible above the surface. The next day at our prayer seminar in Anchorage I explained how prayer should be like those icebergs, with about one-ninth showing in our public group praying and eight-ninths out of sight in secret.

Being close to God

I can almost hear you saying, 'I can't spend great periods of my time shut away.' No, neither can I, but I have found another kind of private praying. It's just being close to God wherever I am – at the kitchen sink, at a desk, or even in a room filled with people.

'You must have tremendous power of concentration,' someone said.

No, I've just learned to draw near to God. Practising this at a California conference with five hundred and twenty-five people packed in a room that barely held five hundred, we found, though touching elbows physically, that we could each draw near mentally to God. This, too, is private praying, though it is no sub-stitute for going to that one spot, at that one time of the day, when we really spend time with God and His Word.

One of my favourite 'places to pray' is my car. You may be sure I don't take my hands off the wheel, fold them, and kneel. To shut my eyes would be even worse!

One morning last week, as I was getting ready to leave for an all-day prayer session fifty miles away, everything went wrong. My husband called from California asking me to find out when certain lecturers should be met at the San Francisco airport, and to give the information to his secretary so he could telephone her after I had gone. I couldn't find the lecturers; I couldn't find the secretary after frantically dialing all the possible numbers.

Then my son telephoned from school: 'Mum, I forgot all my books; could you bring them over?' I did, and was completely out of time when I left his school only to run into such a long traffic diversion that I could hardly find my way back to the main road.

As I finally emerged on the right road, I cried to God, 'O Lord, take over! Remove from me all this tension and frustration. Flow through me with Your peace and power. Make me what You want me to be by the time I arrive at the prayer meeting.' And he did! My car had become my prayer room.

Even a plane seat can be a place of prayer. For two years I had been praying with a friend about her sister who did not know Christ. Every time my friend wrote to her sister, she'd telephone asking me to pray for God to work in her heart as she received the letter. One day my plane had a ten-minute stop over in a city in America's mid-west with no time to disembark. I looked out over that city and thought, *That's where my friend's sister lives!* Suddenly there descended from God a heavy, overwhelming burden to pray for her. I sat in that plane in the very depths of intercessory prayer. Two days later my elated friend called to say, 'I just received a letter from my sister and she accepted Christ!' When? The exact day God had said in that plane, 'Evelyn, pray.'

Which posture?

Just as our 'momentary' praying requires no particular place, neither does it require a certain prayer posture. In one of our seminars a man announced to me after the first session that he would not be back. 'You're not praying scripturally,' he said. When I asked him to please explain, he said, 'You're not "lifting up holy hands."' He could see only this one position to be used at all times even though I pointed out to him that there are many postures of prayer mentioned in the Bible.

Jesus, when He was praying in the garden of Gethsemane, set for us the example of *kneeling* in prayer:

> 'He withdrew about a stone's throw beyond them, *knelt down* and prayed.' (Luke 22:41).

> 'Jesus *looked up* and said, Father, I thank you that you have heard me.'

> 'I want men everywhere to *lift up holy hands* in prayer, without anger and doubting' (1 Tim 2:8).

My husband can recall circumstances in which men experienced such grief and anguish that they have lain prostrate on the floor of his study. One was a dad who had just learned that his unmarried teenage daughter was pregnant. He threw himself to the floor, weeping, and my husband had to take him in his arms and gently lift him up.

King Solomon, in the Old Testament, lay down *before the Lord* when he prayed in the temple. His father, David, spoke with God in his bed (Ps 4:4). Whatever our posture, whatever the place, the ears of our God are attentive to our cry (see Ps 34:15).

Holy places

God does not live in temples made with hands. Even so, some spots have been used for private prayer by so many that they seem to be holy places. Have you ever stepped into a room and felt God there? My husband and I were looking over the grounds at a conference centre last autumn. We stepped into an old chapel –

and I felt God's presence immediately. 'Please go on without me for a few minutes,' I said. I knelt at the altar – not talking or praying, but just *feeling* God so powerfully there.

Another time I arrived at Bethel College in St. Paul to speak at a women's meeting just as the planning committee stepped out of the Eric Frykenberg Prayer Tower, where they had been praying for our meetings. Their eyes were wide with wonder and amazement. 'We felt Jesus in there!'

'Yes,' I replied 'that is one of those places where I always feel a particular sense of the presence of Christ.' That little circular room has no windows, no furniture – but it is filled with the thousands of prayers uttered by students and staff of that college – and His presence!

Christ recognized the need for spending time alone with God. What a tremendous example Christ's prayer life was to His followers and to us. Though the disciples were Jesus' very closest friends, He knew there were times He had to pray in secret to His heavenly Father. So Christ, though He taught His disciples the concept of group prayer, as we have learned in previous chapters, also knew the importance of this private praying. Even though He himself was God incarnate, He thought it necessary to withdraw to a mountain to pray all night alone before the important task of choosing the twelve apostles. If He – why not us?

FOR YOU TO PRAY

'Lord, give me the joy of private praying. Keep me faithful to shut the door every day and spend time with You and Your Word in secret. Teach me to draw apart alone with You, no matter where I am or with whom.'

CHAPTER EIGHT

When to pray

'Pray continually.' 1 Thessalonians 5:17

Did you ever sit in a room before a glowing fire with someone you love? Did you talk every minute? Or did you feel compelled every now and then to clear your throat and say, 'Now dear, I think I'll say something to you.' Then with a bright introduction, did you proceed with a formal speech? Of course not. When you're with a person you love, there need not be a bit of conversation in order for you to experience real communication. If you feel like saying something, you do; if not, you don't, but the line of communication is always open.

Praying without ceasing is like that. How? It's simply turning the dial of our communication system with God to *on,* making possible a two-way conversation with Him at any time. When that communication line is open, we can say whatever we want to Him, and He in turn can say anything He wishes to us. Yes, it's possible to 'pray continually' twenty-four hours a day.

When we leave our daily private praying, do we walk out and slam the door, saying, 'That's it for today! Same time tomorrow, Lord, same channel?' That isn't what the Holy Spirit meant when He inspired Paul to

write, 'Pray continually' (1 Thes. 5:17). Nor is it what
Christ meant when He taught His disciples (Luke
18:1) they should always pray and not give up.

After Paul lists the armour with which we are to
resist Satan, he goes on to say, 'Pray in the Spirit on all
occasions with all kinds of prayers and requests.' (Eph.
6:18). The source of strength in our battle with the
enemy is 'praying always.' But when the line of
communication with God closes, wham – the fiery darts
of Satan strike! But that need not be the case. Let's
break down the day and see how the communication
system between us and God can be open all twenty-
four hours.

A lark or an owl?

How do you start your day? Are you a 'lark' or an 'owl'?
'Larks' twitter and sing in the morning, but by the end
of the day they're not doing too well; they have slowed
down considerably. 'Owls' take a little longer to get
going in the morning. You know – 'Right now I don't
love anybody, but when I start loving again, you'll be
first on the list.' But owls gain momentum as the night
progresses.

We're divided at our house. I'm a 'lark' and my
husband is definitely an 'owl'. When we pray together
at night and Chris prays on and on, I sometimes have
to say, 'Hurry up, Chris; you're losing me.' But in the
morning it's a different story. Chris groans and pulls
the covers up tighter when I shake him to tell him
some great gem that I've just had from the Lord.

Because our individual, inbuilt clocks function
differently, I've learned that there are no spiritual
points to be gained for being a 'lark.' Is it possible our
heavenly Father created some of us to be 'larks' and

some to be 'owls' so He would have somebody on the alert all twenty-four hours of the day?

I used to say, and I'm sure it was with pride, 'I'm creative in the morning. That is my creative time.' Then I realized, *Eve, you're not creative in the morning; you've just learned to listen to God in the early hours.*

When I'm asked, 'How do you get all those talks ready? How can you possibly write so many?' I have to reply, 'I don't write talks, but I keep a little notebook on my bedside table at all times. Then lying there communing with my heavenly Father early in the morning, I just jot down whatever He says to me.'

When I wake up I say, 'Lord, here I am. What do You want to say to me?' I usually think they should be ideas for immediate needs, but frequently He gives thoughts for talks and conferences months away. I write them down and keep them in a file. Then when I put those papers in outline form, it's astounding to learn that God has given me every single thought I'll ever need— in time!

It's a very exciting procedure to wait upon God early in the morning while the mind is fresh, before anyone else comes upon the scene, or before the 'tyranny of the urgent' rushes in. Have you learned to say in the morning, 'Lord, here I am. You tell me what You want me to know today, what You want me to do'? Have you asked Him, 'Is there someone You want me to contact? What do You have in mind for me today?' You'll be amazed at His answers!

One morning as I was lying in bed talking to the Lord, I said, as I frequently do, 'OK, Lord, whom would You have me 'phone today?' The answer came as if it were in lights, 'Mona.'

'But Lord, I don't know Mona. I met her at a concert, and at a PTA meeting – and that's it.'

I waited until the children left for school; then I went to the phone and said, 'Lord, you're going to have to tell me what to say to Mona – I don't know.'

I really felt a little silly about calling her, but I dialed and said, 'Good morning, Mona. This is Evelyn Christenson from down the road.' That's all I said. And Mona started to cry. She told me that the day before, she and her husband had been told by the doctors that their son, Dave (our Jan's friend), had leukemia and would never recover. My obedience gave me the opportunity at least to build a bridge to Mona and to comfort her in her distress.

One morning, after my daughter had asked me to pray for a girl who was feuding with her parents, I said, 'Lord, if You want me to talk to her, have her call or come over.' At two o'clock in the afternoon I answered my doorbell, and there she stood with a suitcase in her hand. 'Hi, I've come to move in with you for a while.'

It had been one of those unbelievably hectic days, and I glanced heavenward and sighed, 'Lord, I didn't mean that *literally.*'

I used to think that if one were an 'owl', talking with God in the morning wasn't necessary. But one day, as I was reading Psalm 5, I saw something for the first time. I said to Chris, 'Hey, it's really scriptural to talk to God first thing in the morning.' In all the times I had read that psalm, it had never really hit me before.

> Give ear to my words, O Lord,
>   consider my sighing.
> Listen to my cry for help,
>   my King and my God,
>   for to you I pray.
> Morning by morning, O Lord,
>   you hear my voice;

morning by morning I lay
my requests before you
and wait in expectation.

(Ps. 5:1–3).

It doesn't say hours of prayer time are necessary, but at least we must say good morning to the Lord and give Him our day. So whether you are a 'lark' or an 'owl', God's word says early in the morning, before the 'tyranny of the urgent,' before breakfast, before the school buses, before anyone says a word to you, 'Early in the morning, Lord, I will look up, and pray to You.'

Prayer before school

After breakfast, it's time for the children to start off to school. Since our first child went to school, we have made a practice in our home of praying individually with each of our children just as they left. This to me has been a very precious experience. It's been more than a time to pray! We have been able to put our arms around our children, assuring them of the security of their home, and then to send them out into the big, often overwhelming world with God watching over them, whatever they will face that day.

Every once in a while I'm told by my son, 'Hurry up, Mum, make it short. The school bus is coming,' and out the door he goes! Sometimes it's only one or two sentences. But meeting God with our family before we separate is a very vital part of our day.

The day progresses

I have a great time with the Lord in the morning. As God and I communicate with one another, He tells me what He wants me to do, and I say, 'OK, Lord.' There are no problems. There aren't any people around to bother me. There are no bad reactions for me to contend with. You know, I could really be a tremendous Christian if I could stay on my own with God. But I can't stay there all day. I can't even remain sheltered with members of my own family, those who love me. I have to get out and meet people – and occasionally my early relationship with God suddenly falls apart!

I'm a 'people person,' and I really like almost everybody I meet. But once in a while somebody makes me bristle, and I retaliate. There are other occasions when I just look at someone and think, 'Oh, brother!'

How do I solve the problem? I've learned what I call my *SOS prayer.* I say, 'Help, Lord.' (But not out loud!) 'Lord, give me the attitude *You* want me to have toward that person.'

Perhaps you can imagine what it's like for a wife and mother to prepare to go out-of-town for a speaking engagement. You get all the washing done, setting out socks and shirts. Then you stock the refrigerator with enough food for all the days you'll be gone, outline each of your talks, try to get yourself and your clothes ready, and do the last-minute shopping. It's really hectic! In addition, you have to get 'prayed up.' You just can't go without spiritual preparation, so you spend extra time with the Lord. Finally you settle into the plane seat, review your notes once more, and pray.

Things had gone that way before I arrived in an eastern city for a conference a few years ago. As I was being introduced to the ladies, a minister's wife who was sitting next to me leaned over and sneered, 'Do you really like these little women's meetings?'

Wow! After all I'd gone through to get there! Besides, I didn't think that meeting was so little – about two hundred were there from several states. And I was all primed and ready to share what the Lord had given me for them. Do you know what I did? I bristled!

Now, I didn't have time to say a long prayer. I had only seconds left before speaking. As I walked to the platform, I silently pleaded with the Lord. *'Help, SOS,* give me the attitude You want me to have toward that minister's wife.' And do you know, all the bristle disappeared. Because God knew I didn't have a lot of time to get this cleaned up, He answered my SOS prayer just like *that!* What would have happened if I had started out bristling at that audience? It would have 'pulled the rug' right out from under the whole conference.

One of the prayer requests presented at a staff wives' prayer meeting I attended several months ago involved a serious financial problem. On the day before, the promise of a large gift of money for the new college had been withdrawn, and we were going to pray about it.

As we were drinking coffee and chatting before the start of the prayer meeting, a woman came in whom I had never met. I didn't know who she was, but I looked down my spiritual nose and thought, *My word, she's the 'squarest' woman I've ever seen in my life.* And the more she talked the more 'square' I thought she was.

Then the Lord began to reprove me: 'Evelyn, that's sin.' Do you remember our first prerequisite to answered prayer? 'If I cherish evil in my heart, the Lord will not hear me'? I suddenly realized that I was about to spend my morning in prayer for these financial needs with sin in *my* heart! Another SOS prayer flew to heaven, 'Lord, please, give me the attitude You want me to have toward that woman, whoever she is.'

You know, when we pray that prayer, we never ask wrongly. God knows what attitude He wants to give us. When we look at Christ's life, we can see that sometimes His perfect attitude was love, sometimes it was righteous indignation, sometimes patience, sometimes discipline, sometimes compassion. That day God gave me a surprise.

Guess who prayed first at that prayer meeting? She did. And as she started to pray, I suddenly realized that this woman had a dimension to her prayer life that I knew nothing about. She said, 'Thank you, Lord, that that money didn't come through yesterday.' And I blinked. She went on, 'Now Lord, You have given us the *privilege* of being humble before You this morning with a desperate need. Lord, what a privilege this is. Thank you, Lord. And thank You that today the college principal has the privilege of being humble before You with this need. Thank You that the whole staff has this tremendous need, and thank You that they have the privilege of being humble before You.'

I felt two inches high.

When I learned who this woman was, I discovered some other things. She had an intercessory prayer life that was never less than two hours a day. She used a prayer list that was pages and pages long, containing the names of the people for whom she prays daily. And *I* had looked at *her* and thought, *Wow, is she 'square!'*

I had a trying experience when I was speaking to wives during a ministers' conference. We had gone over the material on praying in God's will, and were going to have a spiritual exercise by taking partners with whom we would share and pray. My partner was a young minister's wife. We took our chairs to a corner

as we were supposed to, and got all ready for the
spiritual exercise, when suddenly she looked me right
in the eye and said, 'I hate you.'

Do you think I smiled and said, 'Oh, I just love you?'
Not on your life. I said, 'I guess we had better not do our
exercise; we'd better just talk. Tell me why you hate
me.'

But as I was talking outwardly, inwardly I was
praying, 'SOS, Lord. Help me to have the attitude You
want me to have toward this person.' And God gave me
the ability to sit there calmly without becoming angry
and retaliating. 'Would you like to tell me why you
hate me?' I asked.

She said, 'OK, I'll tell you. My husband has been
interviewed by the vacancy committee seeking a
minister for your former church.' She went on, 'I didn't
know who you were when I came to this meeting. I had
never seen you before, had never heard one of your
tapes, but I knew you were the wife of the former
minister of that church.' Then she exploded, 'You're
everything I don't want to be and I can't be in a
minister's wife, so I hate you. Look at that dress you're
wearing,' she said. 'I'm a sweatshirt and jeans girl
myself.'

I was at a loss as to when to start, but God seemed to
be saying to share deeply with her out of my heart. I
told her of the hard things I had talked about in my
message that morning, things that had happened
during my time at that church. I even told her of a very
personal trial I never mention in public, and how those
wonderful people prayed for me – just as they would
pray for her if she were the pastor's wife. It wasn't long
before the two of us were in tears, clasping hands, and
praying together.

As we parted, she said, 'As my husband and I drive

home this afternoon, I want to tell him about how I feel now. Will you pray for me?'

I said I would, but she didn't wait until afternoon. At lunch her husband came flying across the dining room and asked, 'What did you do to my wife?'

I told him I didn't do anything to his wife, but I wanted to know what happened.

He said, 'You know, God is calling me to leave the church I'm now serving, and my wife had been saying 'Absolutely not. I don't care where you're called. I won't go.' But she just came to me and said, 'Darling, wherever God leads you, I'll go along.' What did you do?'

What had I done? I had prayed, 'SOS, Lord. Give me the right attitude toward this woman.' And immediately He had given me an understanding attitude toward a young minister's wife who didn't want to leave her rural community, and her sweatshirt and jeans.

Not long ago a woman stopped me in a church and said, We're going to have a new minister.' Guess who it was? That same young man! Then she went on, 'Do you know why we invited him? He's a great guy, but we were very impressed with his wife. She was so eager to have her husband where God wanted him to be, and she was supporting his ministry as we've never seen any minister's wife do before.' I smiled and breathed a thank-you to God for that little sweatshirt-and-jeans girl who only a year before had said, 'I hate you.'

Carry each other's burdens

How about your family? Is it as easy for your children to say, 'Mum, I'm having a math test at 10.30, please pray,' as it is for them to ask you for their lunch money? Do your children know that your communication system with God is always open?

One morning while she was still at school, one of our daughters was so frightened about an up-coming important interview that I found her being sick in the bathroom. I helped her out the front door and promised to pray. Soon the phone rang. 'Mother, it went great,' she exclaimed, then softly, 'I could *feel* you praying, Mum.'

Our married daughter's father-in-law had just had open-heart surgery. Suddenly the 'Red Alert' was flashed over the hospital intercom. Jan ran to a 'phone, dialed our number, and, with the sounds of running hospital personnel in the background, said, 'Mother, Skip's dad's heart has stopped.'

My heart stood still. I felt so helpless and so far away. 'What can I do?'

There was a long pause, and then she said, 'Just pray, Mother, just pray,' and hung up.

I did pray, and her father-in-law revived and God gave him four more years to live. But the point is that Jan knew she could depend on me to pray about her concerns, any time, any place.

This family prayer support works two ways. After finishing a conference at Mt. Hermon in California, I phoned home long distance. My then 10-year-old son answered with, 'How did it go, Mum?'

Oh, Kurt, it went just great.'

Well, he said with pride in his voice, 'how could you miss with all of us praying for you?'

Do you have someone who will pray for you and for whom you will pray? If you don't know where to start with all these prayer suggestions, find one person with whom you can share the secret problems and needs of your life. Someone who cares and who will never, never

divulge your secrets. Then 'fulfil the law of Christ by
carrying each other's burdens' (see Gal. 6:2).

The Nightwatch

Are you one of these people whom God can awaken in
the middle of the night to pray? 'But I need my sleep,'
you say. So did I, or at least I thought I did. For many
years I was dependent upon sleeping pills. I thought I
had to have eight solid hours of sleep or I'd never make
it the next day. Then one summer day, I very
undramatically tossed those pills into the toilet, flushed
it, and said, "Lord, I'm not going to worry if I'm awake
at night, because if You awaken me, there's a reason
for it. I'll just ask You, 'For whom should I be praying?'"

God knows when I'm finished praying and ready to
go back to sleep. And somehow there's no frustration
and I never miss the sleep when God needs me to pray.
It's a very beautiful, exciting thing.

One night the Lord awoke me and said, 'Pray for
Jacque' (a long-term prayer partner). At that time she
was in San Francisco, and I learned later that she was
going through a very deep spiritual battle, seemingly
surrounded by forces of Satan. A letter Jacque wrote to
me the next morning confirmed the reason God had
awakened me. As I prayed in St. Paul, great peace had
flooded her in San Francisco. *'If at night you can't sleep,
don't count sheep – talk to the Shepherd!'*

Another time I was driving on the motorway in the
state of Wisconsin very late on a Saturday night. It
hadn't occurred to me that my petrol tank might be a
little bit thirsty since I wasn't. All at once, phut, phut,
phut. I was out of petrol! I pulled off the road and
opened the boot (I knew that if I opened the roof, other
motorists approaching from behind would see that

there was a woman alone in a car).

As each set of headlights appeared behind me, I prayed, 'Lord, if there's anybody in that car with whom I won't be safe, keep them going, Lord, keep them going.' I sat there for fifteen minutes, and every set of headlights shot right by. Nobody stopped.

Then I saw a flashing blue light and heard the sound of a siren behind me. For the first time in my life I was happy and excited to hear that sound! The policeman got out of his car and said, 'You know, Lady, that you're in danger out here alone on the motorway this late at night, don't you?

I said, 'Yes, officer, I know.'

He told me that it would take about five minutes to transfer some petrol from his patrol car to mine, and invited me to sit in the squad car. I noticed that he was trembling, and needed desperately to talk to someone.

He said, 'I just came from an accident. A pregnant mother fell asleep, and her car veered off to the right and hit a concrete post. I looked at the car with the right one-third sheared off and thought, *Oh no, this is going to be one of those messy ones.* But the first thing I saw was a little two-year-old girl walking around with just one pulled tendon in her leg. What really unnerved me, though, was that a doll that was placed between the mother and daughter was decapitated by a piece of metal that came through the windscreen, but the two of them were unharmed.' He turned to me and asked, 'Do you believe in God?'

I said, 'Yes.'

Then with deep emotion he said, 'Do you think God was riding in the back seat of that car?'

I replied, 'I think He may very well have been.' Then I added, 'Do you know that you're an answer to prayer, too?'

He said, 'Me? I'm an answer to prayer?'

Then I told him how I had prayed about every single pair of lights approaching my car that night.

This is only a part of the story, and we must go back to Jacque for the end of it, 'Evelyn, why did I feel an overwhelming urgency to pray for you last night? We were having a birthday party and I couldn't pray right then. But again God said, "Jacque, pray for Evelyn." So I gathered up the birthday wrappings, excused myself to take them out, and stood by the dustbin, and prayed.' Then she told me the exact time. Can you guess what time it was? Yes, it was exactly the time I had run out of petrol on the motorway!

Is your communication system so open to God that you are available to pray any time of the day or night? When God sees someone in need, can He say to you, 'Wake up, wake up, I need you to pray for somebody'? Or are you like I was at one time, thinking you need eight hours of sleep or you'll collapse the next day? Are you one of those with whom God can trust His burdens?

'Pray continually' – all day long, all night long. It's just a matter of having the communication system open between yourself and God so you can say at any time of day or night 'SOS', Lord,' And He can say to you, 'There's a need somewhere. Will you please pray?'

FOR YOU TO PRAY

'Dear Father, I want to be available to You twenty-four hours a day. Teach me to open my communication with You and never shut it. Also help me to be available to others whenever they need me to pray.'

CHAPTER NINE

To whom we pray

'Come near to God, and He will come near to you.'
James 4:8

An often overlooked but very important part of prayer is the coming near to God. Before we are ready to start our intercessory prayers, we need to *wait* upon God until we know we have established communication with him. This is a time of silence when we are shutting out every other thought and distraction around us. There is no talking *to* God, just a complete mental coming to Him; and then, as He promised, *He will come near to us.*

Coming near takes time

Coming near to God is important in groups as well as in private praying. It may be easier to do in private; but because of the hectic rush to arrive at a prayer meeting on time or because of the chatting after we've arrived, it is a must to pause for the seconds or minutes it takes to withdraw from all this and draw nigh to God. Often there seems to be embarrassment in a group if someone doesn't start praying audibly right away as we go to prayer – ready or not.

I remember way back in the 'green chair' days struggling and struggling to come near to God. I can recall how I would strain and wonder where He was. And it seemed as if my prayers were only reaching the ceiling. But through the years God has taught me many things – and I'm not in the struggling stage any more.

One thing I learned when I found it impossible to establish communication with God was that it wasn't His fault, it was mine. He is the same yesterday, today, and forever, but I am not. I let sins creep in that break my fellowship with Him, and frequently I must search, my heart and confess those sins that are blocking communication between us.

I also learned the simple process of thinking about my God when approaching Him in prayer. The joy that floods my whole being as I find myself visualizing all God is – all His love, all His power, all His concern for me – defies description. What greater privilege could there be for a human being than to actually come near to the omnipotent, omniscient God, high and lifted up on His throne in glory? This to me is the most precious part of my prayer time.

Be sure it's God

Why do you suppose Christ taught His disciples, and us in turn, to pray, 'Our Father who art in heaven'? Have you ever thought of that? Our God, capital *G*, is the only God in heaven, but there are other gods. 'You shall have no other gods before Me' (Ex 20:3). If there were no other gods, our God would not have given Moses this commandment.

'The god of this world [age]' is a title Paul gives

Satan (2 Cor 4:4). In the explosion of the occult that is sweeping our nation, we are finding that even Christians – real Christians – are getting answers that are not from God. Christ spent a quarter of his recorded ministry dealing with the enemy, and this a warning to us to be constantly alert that we open our minds, not to Satan, but to God who is in heaven.

In a question and answer session at a church youth meeting, following a lecture on the dangers of the occult, a tutor raised his hand and asked, 'Why is it that when I pray I get more answers from Satan than I do from God?'

I didn't want to belittle that man before the students for whom he was responsible, but I had no choice. I looked at him, and I said as kindly as I could, 'Sir, if you are getting more answers from Satan than you are from God, there's something drastically wrong with your prayer-life.'

Is it possible for even sincere Christians unwittingly to open themselves to suggestions from the enemy?

I know of five different ministers who claimed a voice said to them, 'Divorce your wife,' and each one promptly did. They said they thought it was the Lord speaking to them. But it was not surprising to learn that in every instance another woman was involved.

While flying over Canada, one minister said to another, 'I now know there is a life after death and I am preaching it from my pulpit.'

'How do you know?' asked the surprised minister sitting beside him.

'Because my stillborn baby is communicating with me. I wasn't sure before, but I know now there is a life after death!'

When I speak on the occult, I find to my horror that even Christian youth are experimenting with all sorts of occult practices. As I ask them what they do at all night parties, their response is frightening. Many have crossed the thin line between parlour games and the occult. They are hearing voices during their séances, experiencing supernatural power, and getting answers in uncanny ways from Ouija boards.

After I had talked with one group of teenagers in a fine local church, a mother came to me and said, 'I want to tell you that those young people had a Ouija board burning. My daughter is the ringleader of that youth group in our church, and she came home from your meeting and said, "Mother, playing with Ouija boards and all that stuff is detestable to God. It says so in Deuteronomy 18."' Yes, getting supernatural answers through any form of divination or mediums is not coming near to God – and is forbidden by him (Deut 18:9–14).

Halloween parties, too, seem to be changing in character these days. A friend of mine was having her hair done the week after Halloween. Her hairdresser said that every one of her customers who discussed attending any Halloween party said it turned out to be an attempt to come near to spiritual beings other than God. What ever happened to bobbing for apples?

Meditation can be dangerous

Putting oneself into a state of passivity is a very dangerous spiritual exercise in which even true Christians are engaging. To open our minds and allow ourselves to be receptive to all the thoughts and suggestions which enter is a perilous business. We may think that we are coming nearer to God – but all of a sudden there's Satan, and we are listening to *his* voice.

At a prayer conference, a woman came to me and said, 'Do you know that I taught yoga and gave it up?'

I said, 'Tell me, why did you give it up?'

'Well,' she replied, 'I suddenly realized that there I was in that room meditating with Buddhists, with Hindus, with people involved in every religion you can imagine. Sure, you sit there and you meditate and you get a feeling of peace and strength; but I've learned that I get all the peace and strength I need from the Lord Jesus Christ, and I don't need yoga meditation. And God told me it's a sin for me to be meditating with those others who do not know the true God in heaven.'

Oh how foolish to put ourselves in such a vulnerable position! It does make a difference with whom we attempt to draw nigh to God. 'What communion hath light with darkness?' (2 Cor 6:14).

Transcendental Meditation is a guise that Satan frequently uses today to infiltrate minds. It is being taught in many of our schools, libraries, YMCAs, YWCAs, and even in some churches.

While the chairman of a local women's guild and I were driving home together some seventy miles from a meeting, our conversation shifted to communicating. 'You know,' she said, 'I communicate in the middle of the night. Do you?'

'Oh, yes, I communicate in the middle of the night,' I replied.

She went on, 'I know "It" is out there, because I communicate with "It".'

I quickly changed the pronoun and said, 'I know "He" is out there. My God is out there.'

She went on, 'I don't know what it is I'm communicating with, but I know *something* is out there. Why don't you come to one of our meditation meetings? You can tell us how you communicate in the middle of the night, and we can tell you how we do.' By that time I had an ill feeling in my stomach. I couldn't get out of that car fast enough!

Prayer is always directed from us up to God – who is in heaven. This is the vertical dimension of prayer. In the next chapter you will see how this dimension becomes a triangle when God reaches back down to earth with the answers to our prayers.

In Hebrews 11:6 we read that the faith that pleases God is two-faceted:

(1) believing that He exists
(2) believing that He rewards those who earnestly seek Him.

I wonder if Christians before the occult explosion really knew the full meaning of this. Have we concentrated so much on the fact that He is a rewarder that we have lost sight of *who* our God is – holy, high, and lifted up? We must come near to *this* God – and then He will come near to us.

Moses came nearer to God in reality when he went up early in the morning on Mount Sinai (Ex 34:4, 29–35). Do you remember what happened when he came down? The children of Israel were afraid to come near him because the skin of his face shone! He had put a veil over his face, it was so radiant. Wouldn't it be great if we could so draw nigh to God that we would become radiant? So draw nigh that others could tell by our very expression that we had been with God? That we had learned the secret of His presence? That before bombarding Him with our requests, we had taken time to enter into His fellowship?

FOR YOU TO DO

Before starting to pray, in absolute silence practise coming near to God.

This may involve confessing some sin which God brings to your mind. If so, confess it, so that there is nothing between you and God in heaven.

Now come near to Him. *Wait in silence until you feel God is there.*

Now pray, *thanking God for who He is – whatever you want to say in adoration and praise for who He is – this God to whom you have just come near.*

Now pray *at least one request for some other person's need.*

CHAPTER TEN

The results of prayer

'Without faith it is impossible to please God, because anyone who comes to Him must believe that He exists and that He rewards those who earnestly seek Him.'
Hebrews 11:6

With the study of the horizontal dimension of prayer, we now reach full circle. We have said that we cannot pray effectively when there is sin in our lives. We have described how to pray in God's will so that our prayers will be answered. We have spoken of the need to come near to God, and to bask in the sunshine of His love because He never makes a mistake.

For what purpose have we taught about these prerequisites to prayer? Primarily, that we might become powerful in intercessory prayer. We are now back to the theme verse of chapter one. 'The prayer of a righteous person is powerful and effective.' (James 5:16).

The horizontal dimension of prayer is the visible result of our effective praying here on earth. But there can never be a horizontal dimension of prayer unless there is first the vertical dimension – that coming near to God. The two are inseparable, standing as it were at the opposite points of the base of a triangle, with God at the top. When we pray, we petition God the Father, who receives the prayer, sifts it out according to His will, then reaches down to change people and circumstances on earth. *The results we see represent the horizontal dimension of prayer.*

Unity

In chapter one I gave many illustrations to show what happens when women pray. Each was a visible result, on the horizontal level, of prayer that had ascended to God the Father, who in turn acted upon an individual or a set of circumstances here on earth. I also mentioned the tremendous unity that was experienced as members of the body of Christ prayed together. It is still happening.

Following the day of humiliation, fasting, and prayer for our country on April 30, 1974, I received telephone calls from several prayer group members. One woman said, 'It was just beautiful in our group.'

Another exclaimed, 'Guess what? We finally got off the ground for the first time, really off the ground, and we're going to meet next month again, just as we did on April 30th.'

Another said, 'We had the most beautiful experience. I helped our minister organize the prayer meetings in our church. We used the six S's and prayed in groups of four. It was a fantastic experience.'

What else happened to many of us that day? We sensed deeply the humiliation about which we had prayed. With the continuing exposure of the Watergate affair, we knew that God was bringing us as individuals and our nation as a whole to the place of humility. And we felt a tremendous unity not as we studied together, or talked, or met as committee members, but as we prayed together. One definite horizontal result of prayer, then, is unity – in the church, in the home, and in the community.

Prayer transcends miles

Do you have loved ones who live a great distance from you? Perhaps a son or a daughter who is away at school? Between my mother and me lies the entire state of Wisconsin, and beyond that the vastness of Lake Michigan. Yet in prayer we both sense a oneness that transcends the miles that separate us. God is not limited to space, as we are. He is able to reach down and give the unifying sense of His presence not only to people sitting beside us in the room but to individuals who are separated by continents. We proved this by an experiment in 1965.

After I had been praying with my two prayer partners Lorna and Sig every Thursday afternoon for almost a year, my husband and I went overseas to visit the mission fields. Before leaving we noted when we were scheduled to land in Addis Ababa, Ethiopia (where Sig's daughter Shirley and her son-in-law Cliff were posted). Our arrival would be just prior to the corresponding time that Lorna and Sig would be meeting for prayer in Rockford, though there would be an eight-hour difference on the clock. We calculated that if all the planes were on schedule and if everything went according to plan, we would be in Addis Ababa to pray with Sig's daughter and her husband at exactly the same time Sig was praying with Lorna in Rockford.

Having slept only two out of four nights en route, we arrived in Addis Ababa exhausted, but on schedule.

All the guests went to bed except me. After the house was quiet, Cliff, Shirley and I went to prayer in the living room. We had prayed for a short while when suddenly each of us had an overwhelming sense that no miles separated us and the two prayer partners back in Rockford. It was just as if they were right there praying with us. God had transcended all the miles-across half the continent of the United States, the entire Atlantic ocean, and most of the continent of Africa, and given to us a sense of oneness in His Spirit through prayer.

After we returned home, I was anxious to learn what had happened in Rockford that Thursday afternoon. Had they felt that oneness that transcends the miles? Sig said to me then, and she has repeated it ever since, 'Eve, I have never in all my years as a Christian been so aware of God and His power, so aware of His reality, as I was when I sensed that tremendous unity we had in Him, even though we were separated by thousands of miles.' This, too, is the horizontal dimension of prayer, linking us as we pray through our omnipresent God.

We had never met

Closely related to the transcendence of miles is the bond created by prayer even among people who have never met. In 1968 one of the ladies in our prayer-chain went to another state to purchase a poodle from a woman we knew only as Joy. Joy had had an operation involving the insertion of a plastic esophagus, and was having an extremely difficult pregnancy. It was no wonder that our prayer-chain member came back and said, 'Let's pray for Joy.' We started, and week after week, month after month, we prayed for her.

One day, after Joy had her baby, she told her husband

that it was only because those women down there in Rockford were praying that she had the strength and the courage to get through her pregnancy. And that was not all – this dear woman accepted Christ as her personal Saviour, and became the best missionary we ever had! Everyone who came to buy a poodle heard that she had found Christ, and was told about the women many miles away who had prayed and prayed for her physical and spiritual needs. I haven't met Joy to this day. It isn't likely that I will, for I don't think I'll ever buy a poodle. But God answered anyway!

On our prayer-chain lists are many whom we have never met, but God knows who they are and where they are. He knows their needs. All we do is pray our requests – we don't pray answers – and God with the mighty arm of His power reaches down to anyone anywhere on earth with His answer.

God rewards . . .

Much happens when we pray. And answers come as we pray in faith believing. As I mentioned in the previous chapter,

> 'Without faith it is impossible to please God, because anyone who comes to Him must believe that He exists and that He rewards those who earnestly seek Him.'
> (Heb 11:6).

We come first of all believing that He exists, and then believing unequivocally that 'He rewards those who earnestly seek Him.'

As we pray believingly, we see a fourth result in the horizontal dimension of prayer – *it is great in its working*. We are not dropping our prayers into a bottomless pit. How do we know? One way is by the specific answers to specific requests.

We began to experience great answers to prayer early in our prayer ministry. At the very first conference in White Bear Lake, a woman handed me a request for our intercessory prayer time. It was for her sister to receive Christ. She said, 'We've tried everything we know. We've talked to her; we've taken her to meetings where she's spurned invitation after invitation to receive Him. Please pray.' Though they did not even know her name, two hundred and fifty women homed in on that unsaved sister.

The next week the woman who had requested prayer stopped me before the session. 'Do you know what? I took my sister to a Christian Women's luncheon right after the session last week, and she accepted Christ within two hours of your praying! Those two hundred and fifty who had prayed gave great praise during prayer-time that day.

One morning we missed one of our prayer group committee members. Someone said, 'She's taking her mother, who has tuberculosis, to the hospital.'

Another woman suggested immediately, 'Let's stop right now and pray.'

To that another committee member added, 'But that isn't her mother's greatest need. Neither her mother nor her father knows Christ as Saviour.'

Instead of doing much planning that morning, we spent most of the time praying for the mother and father of our committee member. A couple of weeks after the seminar was over, still another member of the steering committee stopped me on the street and asked, 'Eve, did your hear the good news? Do you know that within two weeks after the prayer group committee prayed, both the mother and father found

Christ?' In just two weeks! 'The prayer of a righteous man is powerful and effective.' (James 5:16).

At a recent prayer session we prayed very definitely that a certain woman would find Christ. That very night she received Him as her Saviour. In the same week we had another answer. A mother was called out of one of our seminars because her little boy had injured his leg at school and couldn't stand on his foot. We promised to pray during the intercessory prayer time. When he was told that all those women had prayed for him, he said, 'Then I must be OK.' He threw away the ice pack they had put on, and went riding off on his bicycle!

God gave us a beautiful answer to prayer last year. We had learned that a young woman of twenty-three with two children had a cancerous growth on her brain. It was the type that had spread like the tentacles of an octopus, and her doctors gave her only a few weeks to live. All of us in the seminar went to prayer for this young mother, not just praying that she would be healed, but that God's will would be done in her life. In this instance God chose to heal this young woman. A few weeks later, we learned that the tumor was shrinking rapidly and that there was not a sign of a cancerous cell in her whole body. The doctors had given her a normal life expectancy!

What happens when we pray? Things do happen. We do not drop our intercessory prayers into a bottomless pit. We send them up to a heavenly Father, who in His time, in His way, according to His will, answers them down here on earth.

Requests change

We see something else taking place in the horizontal dimension of prayer – we begin to see changes in our prayer requests. In 1968, when our prayer experimentation started, several in our denomination were trained in Washington, D.C. for the Crusade of the Americas. We returned to our homes all excited over the prospects of prayer and evangelism. I said to my husband, 'We're going to pray for a year and then we're going to evangelize for a year.'

He grinned and announced, 'It'll never work.'

Jolted, I asked, 'Why not?'

He replied, 'You show me someone who's praying and I'll show you somebody who's evangelizing. A praying church is an evangelizing church.'

He was right! Our objective had been to pray in 1968, and to evangelize in 1969. But when the time came for my report to our national committee in June, 1969, I had to say, 'The transition has already taken place.'

We found that people who prayed automatically evangelized; they naturally shared their Christ with somebody else. With prayer chains praying for each of them, we developed thirty-five evangelism Bible studies in our church, in homes, offices, and in high school, among women, couples, and young people. A Bible study group entirely composed of hippies was studying regularly as a result of Arthur Blessit's meeting that year. New converts had already opened their homes and become teachers for their evangelism Bible studies. We had participated in the distribution of Gospels to every home in our city.

In my 1969 report, I said, 'We are seeing our total church programme becoming increasingly evangelistic, not superimposed by programmes, but from within the hearts of the workers. . . . Our local church has been the greatest recipient of the blessings because we, as the pilot church, have put into practice the prayer ideas of the committee before they were passed on as being workable.'

Are you concerned about outreach in your own life? In your church? When you have a praying life and a praying church, I guarantee you will have a life and a church with a vital outreach, because as we learn to pray, our prayer requests change.

It's interesting to go back and look at the careful notes I made in those months in 1968 when we first started to pray. I notice particularly that one had to have a broken leg or something equally serious to be included on our prayer lists! If we could see the need with our physical eyes – if it needed a bandage or plaster – we gave the request to our prayer-chain. Otherwise it didn't get very much attention.

Gradually, though, things have changed. As our spiritual eyes began to open, we saw spiritual needs and added these to our lists. God in heaven is concerned about physical needs. He expects us not only to pray about them but to add actions to our prayers, to take someone a meal, or to help in any other way we can. But we aren't to stop there. We need to ask God to open our spiritual eyes that we might see the spiritual needs around us, especially in the lives of people who need to be transformed by Christ. This is the greatest need of every person on earth. But how can we share these prayer requests with others?

Prayer partners

After a luncheon at which I had shared the horizontal blessings of a prayer ministry, a woman came to me with tears in her eyes. She said, 'I'm overwhelmed; there's so much to remember. Where do I start?'

I told her that beyond her own personal praying, the place to start intercessory prayer is with *one prayer partner*. This is the best way I know. Find someone with whom you can share big things and little things. When you hurt or have a headache, when some little thing goes wrong or when the whole world collapses around you, have one person you can trust absolutely, and upon whom you can call at any time. Find someone who will not betray your confidence, someone who is always ready to say whenever you 'phone her, 'I'll pray right now.' Then, as you pray together, start praying for what God wants you to do for your church, family, those in need. And then be open to those God would have pray with you.

Church lists

As our intercessory prayer develops on the horizontal level through private praying and prayer partners and prayer groups, we can proceed to church lists. One church in which we held a meeting encourages members of the congregation to fill out a form early in the Sunday morning service. It reads, 'During our prayer time this morning, I would like my brothers and sisters in Christ to pray for . . .' Following several blank spaces there is room for the signature of the person making the requests. These sheets are collected, and the pastor remembers the specific requests in his morning prayer.

The members of another congregation place their prayer requests on registration cards during the morning service. Later in the day these requests, along with other items for praise, are listed on sheets which are distributed in the evening service. These are beautiful examples of members of the body of Christ praying for one another and bearing one another's burdens as members of Christ's family.

Prayer calendars

Prayer calendars represent another method of systematic prayer on the horizontal level. Usually two categories are covered – people and events. An individual may have a particular need on a certain day, or there may be a public meeting or an evangelistic effort which demands definite prayer. These requests may be on local or a national level.

In 1968, in a circle of less than thirty women, we placed our names on a prayer calendar. Each woman prayed for a different woman each day so every person in that circle was prayed for daily. It was exciting. We heard women say, 'I could feel you praying; my life was different when I knew that I was being supported and undergirded specifically by somebody in my circle.'

There can be any number of variations in prayer calendars. Include missionaries, your pastor and church staff, youth ministries, and special projects. It is a great spiritual exercise.

Yes, when we started experimenting with all these methods of intercessory prayer in 1968, I wondered if anything would happen, if there would be any horizontal results. I'm not wondering any more. I know that the prayer of a righteous person is powerful and effective, and I know it from experience.

FOR YOU TO PRAY

1 **Ask God** *to give you the next step He has for you in prayer – a prayer partner (ask for a specific name), a group He wants you to join or start, or a new method of prayer for your church group, family, or youth club.*

2 **Wait** *in silence for Him to speak.*
2 **Promise** *Him you will start immediately whatever He is telling you to do.*

CHAPTER ELEVEN

Forgiveness through prayer

'And forgive us our sins, just as we have forgiven those who have sinned against us.' Matthew 6:12 (LB)

A horizontal dimension of prayer that Christ taught is frequently overlooked by those seeking a deeper prayer life. And it relates to the thing that is *most apt to break up your prayer group* – your relationship with the other people who are in that group!

In the Lord's Prayer we read, 'And forgive us our sins *as* we forgive those who sin against us' (Matt 6:12). Your Bible translation may say debts or transgressions, but both have the same literal meaning: sins. Now, this is the Lord Jesus Himself teaching the disciples, and us in turn how to pray. If you want to keep your prayer group intact, practice this principle.

That word *as* is a conditional word meaning 'to the extent that' – to the extent that I forgive others, I'm asking God to forgive me.

Christ explained it like this in the two verses which follow the Lord's Prayer:

For if you forgive men when they sin against you, your heavenly Father will also forgive you. But if you do not forgive men their sins, your Father will not forgive your sins. (Matt 6:14–15).

Do you remember our first prerequisite to answered prayer in chapter one, 'If I regard iniquity in my heart, the Lord will not hear me'? (Ps 66:18) Christ says that if we don't forgive others, our heavenly Father will not forgive us. If He does not, our sins will keep Him from hearing our intercessory prayers. They will be of no avail.

So, unless we keep our relationships with other people clear, we cannot be effective in intercessory prayers. Now, let's remember one more thing from chapter one: God always hears the penitent sinner's prayer as he confesses his sins and seeks Christ as his Saviour. God also hears the plea for forgiveness of sins by the one who is already a Christian. But for us to refuse to forgive others is itself a sin. We can't be right with God and effective intercessors if we harbour the sin of an unforgiving spirit – even though we may have confessed all *other* known sins. This is a very difficult lesson for some to learn, but it is very important.

At another time while teaching His disciples to pray in faith, Jesus admonished them in rather strong words,

'Listen to Me! You can pray for anything, and if you believe, you have it; it's yours! But – when you are praying, first forgive anyone you are holding a grudge against, so that your Father in heaven will forgive you your sins too' (Mark 11:24–25, LB).

Dealing with those who cause grief

I want to share with you the way this truth was brought into focus for me in the summer of 1972. I was all set to

speak at a prayer breakfast for holiday-makers and
women from several churches in Michigan. It was
possible that some people present would not know
Christ, so I first made a telephone call to the leader of a
local prayer-chain and gave her my request. She jotted
it down and indicated that she would be happy to take
care of the whole thing. Still feeling the need for special
prayer, I called another local chain and then phoned
long distance back to my former prayer-chain in Rockford for their support.

When I got back home, I called the prayer-chains to
send through praise for God's blessing at the prayer
breakfast. The leader to whom I spoke during my first
call was very quiet for a minute. Then she said, 'Er . . .
we didn't pray.'

I exclaimed, 'You didn't pray!'

'No,' she replied, 'one of the members said, "We don't
pray for speakers on this prayer-chain."'

I was stunned, and I gathered that this woman was
seeing prayer needs only with her physical eyes, not
with her spiritual eyes, for this was a spiritual need.
This person who had enough authority to prevent a
prayer from going through an entire prayer-chain
stopped it dead – and no one received the request.

How did I react? Just like a human being. I admit it
was wrong, but I was very upset for several days. And
my spiritual life? I can only explain it by saying it
became just like pulp. If you want your prayer group to
fall apart, to become like pulp, just become angry with
another person in the same way I did.

Soon after this incident, Chris and I took a holiday
9,000 feet up in the Rocky Mountains. It should have
been a beautiful time of fellowship with God, but I
couldn't get through to Him in prayer. My Bible reading
was meaningless; my whole spiritual life still felt like

pulp. I was hollow inside and feeling perfectly miserable.

Finally, by Thursday of that week, I had had it. At five a.m. I grabbed my Bible, went out under those gorgeous pine trees, knelt by an old pine log, and cried out to God, 'Show me what's wrong with my life. I can't get through to You.'

I flicked through the pages of my Bible, but found nothing that suited my need. Then in desperation I turned another page, and my eyes fell on the words right at the bottom of a page, 'If anyone had caused grief.' *Why, Lord, that's what's wrong with me*, I thought. *I've been grieved*. Then God spoke to me: 'Why don't you read on.' I read on – and, wow, what I discovered was a *formula* to remedy my ailment.

I remember the exact page in my Bible – it was 1,253 – where God met me. This prescription was for me as an individual, and it's also for you as an individual, and for your prayer group as well. It will keep your prayer group and your prayer-chain intact. The scripture passage is 2 Corinthians 2:5–11.

'But if any have caused grief . . .' (v. 5). Yes, this woman had caused me grief all right! Though I was innocent, I was still grieved – and miserable.

'The punishment inflicted on him by the majority is sufficient for him.' (v. 6).I suddenly realized that she was being shunned not only by me, but by others who had learned of her refusal to let my prayer request be put on the prayer-chain. The news had got round.

'Now instead, you ought to forgive . . .' (v. 7). I saw that I had to forgive. You see, God wasn't hearing my prayers. I had asked Him for forgiveness. but I hadn't forgiven the person who had upset me. So I prayed, 'Father, give me the strength to forgive this person.' He did, and I forgave her at that point.

'*And comfort . . .*' (v. 7). I was shocked, I knew that word comfort meant encouragement plus alleviation of grief. 'But, Lord,' I said, '*I'm* the one who's been grieved, I'm supposed to alleviate *her* grief? Lord, you have something turned around.'

'No,' He said, 'you are supposed to comfort, encourage, and alleviate the grief so that she will not be overwhelmed with excessive sorrow'" (v. 7).

'Lord, do you mean that the person who has grieved me might have a reason for acting that way? Maybe she feels threatened? Maybe she's finding the going hard?'

I could hear Him say, 'Right.'

If someone is grieving us, how many of us take the wrong attitude? Though we may not say it in so many words, by our manner we are saying, 'I know you're drowning, but I'll just take my foot and push you under to be sure you go down well.' Aren't we guilty of this? But God's word says we are to get underneath, alleviate, and lift! Then, after we do that, we are to:

'*Re-affirm your love for him*'(v. 8). I began to see that I had no love. Oh, I might have had a little supply of the ordinary love that one has for the members of her church – you know the kind I mean. But it wasn't any special love – there was none of that. In fact, it might have been something just the opposite right then. I'm not sure what I felt, but I know it wasn't deep Christian love.

Then I had to pray, 'Lord give me the love You want me to have for this person.' And kneeling by that old log, I suddenly had a tremendous sense of God's love being poured upon me. There it was – and I loved her.

But there was a new problem: how to 're-affirm it.' I couldn't get myself to write a letter, but when I reached home I was still convinced that I had to re-affirm my love to her.

The woman who had aggrieved me attended the same church as I did. (Chris is now Assistant Vice-Principal of Bethel College and is not in the regular ministry, so we were attending as members, not as minister and wife.) On the first Sunday morning we were back in church, I spied her sitting on the opposite side of the church. I didn't hear one word the minister said as I kept praying, 'Lord, if You want me to confirm this love, You have to put her right where I'm going to run into her. I'm not going to make a fool of myself and run over to her.'

You know how that kind of prayer goes. Maybe I didn't get quite that aggressive, but that's what I was saying to God: 'I'm not going to make a fool of myself. You're going to have to put her in my path.' And so help me! At the close of the service I opened the big double doors at the back of the sanctuary and almost knocked her down! There she was!

And what did I have to do? I put my arms around her and said only one thing, 'I just want you to know I love you.' And the tears started to roll.

She said, 'And I just want you to know that my husband and I are praying for your Bible study.'

She 'knew' and I 'knew.' We got together and really worked it out a few days later.

'. . . *to see if you would stand the test and be obedient in everything.' (v. 9).* Why did I have to go to her? '. . . to see if you would stand the test . . .' – you the member of the prayer group who has been upset, the innocent member of the prayer group, who is responsible to forgive and go and confirm his or her love so that God will know how big a person you are – not the one who did the upsetting, but the innocent one who has been upset.

'In order that Satan might not outwit us' (v. 11). This is the most frightening thing of them all. There is nothing the enemy would rather do than to see our prayer groups broken up by our failure to forgive and confirm love. Let's never be guilty of allowing him to 'get his foot in the door,' for we are not ignorant of his devices.

This is for everybody

I had spoken to a group on this subject of forgiveness, and following the morning service that day, a leading layman who had been listening said to me, 'I just want you to know that two men in our church got together afterwards and resolved something that had been between them for many years, and should have been sorted out years ago.'

A man who attended one of our seminars had lent a relative some money, even though he could hardly spare it. He shared his feelings with me after our session on forgiving others. 'Evelyn,' he said, 'I just told God that I now forgive the one who borrowed that money a couple of years ago and has not even mentioned it to me since. I was becoming more and more bitter in my heart, and I now know that I have to go and re-affirm my love to that relative. So when I get home tonight, I'm going to dig out the I.O.U., write on it 'Paid', and put it in the post straight away.'

FOR YOU TO DO

Ask God to bring to your mind that person who has upset you and whom you have not forgiven.

Pray *and ask God to forgive you for the sin of not forgiving that person.*

Now forgive *that person, asking God to give you the strength and ability if you need to.*

Now ask God *for as much love as He wants you to have for that person who upset you.*

Next ask God *how you should re-affirm your love to that person.*

Wait in silence *for His answer.*

Pray, *promising God that you will do whatever He has told you.*

Go and do it!

CHAPTER TWELVE

Telephone
prayer-chains

'Do not be anxious about anything, but in everything, by prayer and petition, with thanksgiving, present your requests to God' Philippians 4:6

What I missed most when I moved from Rockford, Illinois in the autumn of 1970 was the one hundred and fifteen women who prayed for me on the telephone prayer-chains. Every time I spoke, every time I was ill, every time there was a need in my family, these women prayed. I, of course, was not the only one for whom they interceded. There were hundreds of others whose physical and spiritual needs were brought before God.

For a long time after we moved to Minnesota, I kept a hot line going to Rockford with requests for the prayer-chains. There were those who prayed like this in my new home area, but I hadn't found them yet. I no longer need to 'phone Rockford as often for there are many active prayer-chains in our area now!

You don't have to be told that I believe strongly in prayer-chains. They are very close to my heart since I depend almost entirely on the answers God gives them when they go to prayer, and I act accordingly. When everyone is praying simultaneously for the same requests, there is really tremendous power in prayer. I know that great changes have taken place in my life because the prayer-chains have prayed for me.

Power over the enemy

When I first started to speak against the occult, for example, I began to experience some horrible inner feelings. At times after speaking I was so filled with resentment and anger that I actually wanted to kick my car! Members of my family remarked that I was a different person when I spoke on that subject, Why was this so? Because I was intruding in Satan's realm. Then I took the advice of one of the leading Christian authorities on the subject of the occult, and formed a ten-member prayer-chain from among the strongest praying Christians I knew.

The very next time I went out to speak on this subject, all those negative feelings had disappeared. Since that prayer-chain was activated, I have had nothing but a victorious experience each time I have spoken against the occult.

Personal needs

Before leaving for meetings in another state, I asked several prayer-chains to be praying at the exact hour when I would be appearing on a television programme. After I completed one speaking engagement at a lunch for Christian women, I was whisked across town to the television studio to take part in the second half-hour of the programme. Arriving during the commercial break I was not aware that a spurious preacher from Korea had just preceded me on the programme. Had I known this, I would have been completely unnerved. Instead I chatted enthusiastically on the subject of prayer – how, when, and where God answers. Friends who watched both half-hours of that programme told me the astounding difference there was between them. God had guarded me – beause of all those simultaneous prayers.

I have a folder bulging with recorded prayer requests and answers that were handled through our Rockford prayer-chains. As I reviewed these in preparation for the writing of this book, I was overwhelmed at the number of times my name appears – on an average of four times a week! There were requests for my speaking engagements, for physical strength, and for help at times when I was ministering for Christ. Here's one example: 'April 14: Pray for strength for Evelyn. She has the 'flu, and is down to speak at Janesville tonight. The women want to learn about prayer-chains and how to pray effectively.'

'April 15: Evelyn made the meeting. Her talk was much appreciated. Many ladies were touched by God and eager to be changed.' It was always understood that they were to pray that God would make me well enough to go if it was His will that I be there.

You may feel that you could not have such a prominent place in the prayer concerns of a large group. Perhaps that it true. I have a wonderful privilege to be prayed for so much. Nevertheless, you can reap benefits by finding just one or two prayer partners and praying regularly for and with one another. But remember, my prayer-chains started with just eight members. Why don't you start one?

A lesson for the family

One exceptional thing about prayer-chains is what they do for your home. If you want to really teach prayer to your children, I know of no better way than prayer-chain procedures.

As the children hear their mother 'phoning through the prayer requests, and then watch as she bows her head immediately after putting down the receiver, they know that she believes in prayer. When the answer comes through they can hear her say, 'Oh, that's great!' They watch her as she dials the next person on the prayer-chain, and they listen as she says, 'Praise God. He answered our prayer.' They take note of her joy as she bows her head and thanks God for answering.

As prayer-chain calls come into the home, the children and other members of the family can observe the progress of prayer, taking note of specific requests, specific answers, God's timing, and the flow of praise.

For our family, this has been one of the greatest lessons through all the years of bringing up our children. They believe so much in prayer-chains that both our daughters, when they were out of town, have spent their own money to 'phone long-distance with requests. Now our son, Kurt, the only child still living at home, every once in a while comes out with, 'I think it's time to call the prayer-chain!'

Once while Kurt and I were painting the ceiling of our verandah, the telephone rang, but I wasn't in any particular hurry to answer – you know how it is – being up a ladder and with the paint dripping down my arms! Our daughter Nancy picked up the kitchen phone, and, in a few seconds she called in, 'Never mind, Mother, it's *just* another answer to prayer.'

Nancy herself was a subject for prayer on her wedding day. The note from my file reads: 'June 8 – 6.30 p.m. Chris 'phoned the prayer-chain with a specific request: "Pray for Nancy who is vomiting and has diarrhoea. Pray for God's divine healing as she is being married today."'

The entry on June 9 reads: 'Praise the Lord. Nancy was a bit queasy in the tummy, but came through in fine shape for the wedding!'

In Rockford we had an amusing illustration of the way children are impresssed by the prayer-chains. Our children's worker, Gail, was teaching prayer to a group of young people. While meeting one Saturday, Gail said to the youngsters, 'Would you please pray for the minister's wife? She's speaking in Chicago today.'

Just then a little boy raised his hand and said, 'Never mind. You know that thing, that prayer-chain thing? They've already prayed. It's all done.'

Prayer-chains provide a wonderful method of teaching complete confidence in answered prayer. Let your children hear these specific answers that are reported over your telephone. It will do something for your entire family.

Not only mothers, but whole families are involved in the ministry of prayer chains. I remember one Sunday in Rockford a well-known Gospel singer and his family were visiting his parents. He is paralyzed from the waist down, and on that particular day his urinary tract stopped functioning. By 6 pm the family was quite alarmed and had telephoned the hospital to say they'd bring him in.

As they were ready to leave for the hospital, his mum said, 'Let's try the prayer-chain first.' At six-twenty, when everybody was scurrying around getting ready for the evening church service, the prayer-chains were activated. The request could not have come at a better time; everybody was home. Members of whole families stopped what they were doing and prayed for him. Later his mother said, 'A very amazing thing happened. While the prayer-chains were praying, suddenly, it was just as though an electric shock whizzed right through our house, and through my son's body. We didn't have to take him to the hospital because his whole system started to function normally once again.'

Church families, too

Another beautiful illustration of family involvement was the result of a request dated Sunday, March 23rd: 'Please pray for Becky. She has started labour pains. The baby is not due for seven or eight weeks.' (Becky is the one mentioned in an earlier chapter whose first child was lost through a cot death.) That morning, before Sunday service, one hundred and twenty homes received this specific request through the prayer chains. Mothers, fathers, and children all stopped to pray.

Later, the burden was shared with the whole church family and they all joined in prayer for Becky. The record made on Monday, March 24th, reads: 'Pray for Becky, and especially for her 3 lb., 8 oz. daughter.' On Tuesday, March 25th, the request was urgent: 'Becky's baby has developed lung complications. Pray that God's strength will sustain Becky and Eddie, that the God who never makes a mistake will do what is best.' God worked in a wonderful way.

Becky and I belonged to the same circle in our church, Every month she brought that healthy, happy little 'answer to prayer' to our meetings and set her on a blanket in the middle of the floor – what a precious reminder of God's ability to answer prayer!

Felt in hospitals

Many prayer-chain requests are for those who are in hospital. I have one note in my folder which reads: 'Alice went to see Inez, who remarked, "Your friends must be really praying. God was so near to me, and I'm not afraid any more." Her tests show a malignancy, and the nurses and the other patients can't understand the change in her attitude. She tells them God did it, and she's not afraid any more.'

There was also praise from Florence: 'I'm so thankful God took me through this last experience. I was never more conscious that He was near. Each day I felt upheld by your prayers.' As we received thank-you notes and telephone calls from patients for whom we prayed, most of them said, 'I could feel you praying.'

In Bible study groups

Some of the most exciting answers to our prayer-chain praying have come out of Bible study groups. There was Lynn, for example. She had threatened to break up our meeting the first time she attended one of my Bible studies. She stood on her head, showing us how *she* had learned to meditate in her search for answers to life. Our prayer-chains were already praying for her, and Lynn found Christ when she attended the Bible study the second time. After receiving Him she said to me, 'I want to be on the prayer-chain that prayed for me.' Immediately she requested prayer for her friend, Sandy, to find Christ. Then came the day when she called, full of excitement, 'Sandy has accepted Christ!' After a long pause, she said, 'Now I'll have to find somebody else to put on the prayer-chain.'

Do you believe that thoroughly in prayer, in answers to prayer? Lynn does.

Among my notes, I have a request dated March 19th, pertaining to groups that meet over coffee: 'Lee would like us to pray for the seven Bible studies this morning and others this afternoon. Pray especially that the Holy Spirit will convince them of the need for salvation.' The answer: 'Four found Christ that day!' One of the requests our prayer-chains honoured every day was to pray specifically for those attending the Bible studies.

Courses

Recently I received a call from the chairman of one of our previous prayer courses. It illusrates the way prayer-chains grow out of these sessions. She said, 'This is the week you're going to teach prayer-chains in your present five-week course, isn't it?' I told her it was. Then she went on, 'Well, I'm leaving for California, but I want you to know what we have done in our area. We have just started six prayer-chains, and we have almost enough people to form a seventh. We have three morning chains, an evening chain, and an emergency chain that operates around the clock. Both men and women take part in this one. And we average three to nine requests per day on those prayer-chains.'

I then asked, 'What's happening?'

She answered, 'We're taking requests for physical and spiritual problems, from those who are having difficulties in their homes, and we're seeing things cleared up with beautiful answers to prayer. This is the most exciting thing that has come out of our prayer-seminar. We're finding a unity among people from all the different churches that are represented on our prayer-chains, and we feel this is a real service to the Lord.'

The woman who ran our conference in California wrote, 'Prayer-chains are springing up all around now – men's, women's, and even children's prayer-chains!' Prayer-chains are not just for women. It's exciting to see everyone in a church involved – the minister, members of the various committees – everybody. The host at one of our prayer conferences started an all-men's prayer-chain with a challenge to the men in one of his church groups. 'You know,' he said, 'there are certain things I cannot give to women to pray about. I need some men volunteers.' He got them – one hundred per cent!

A national youth speaker telephoned and said, 'I just listened to your prayer tapes while I was driving from Michigan to Pennsylvania. Now I feel that I wouldn't dare go through these fourteen speaking engagements where I'll be bringing messages against the occult without prayer.' We prayed, and when I next heard from him, he wrote, 'I could feel you praying and I never before had such freedom, such attentiveness, and discipline in the schools where I spoke.'

The Chairman

In Rockford we had ten prayer-chains with ten or so persons on each chain. Because we wanted to have as many people as possible praying simultaneously, our chairman, after receiving the calls and recording the requests verbatim, called person number one on all ten of the prayer-chains, and in fifteen minutes one hundred and fifteen people were praying.

Incoming prayer requests may come from any source, but it's important that only the bare essentials be communicated in the request. A discerning leader will sense when something is too personal, and will ask, 'Have you checked with the person for whom you're requesting prayer?' As I look over the recorded requests in my folder I am amazed at the spiritual insight of our leader and the careful wording she used in the prayer requests. For years she had helped me with housework, and we had spent many hours in prayer together. But there came the day when after much surgery, she could no longer do housework and felt that God was calling her to be our prayer-chain leader.

When she accepted the position, she stood up in our women's meeting and said, 'I thank God for all the pain and the surgery, for He has shown me that there's something much greater that I can do for Evelyn than ironing and making cakes.'

No gossiping

A testimony by one of our prayer recipients attests to the strong commitment of our prayer-chain members. It happened that the woman in whose house we had our Bible study for three years had a daughter who had left home and strayed far from Christ. Through her broken marriage, a divorce, and her remarriage, our prayer-chains kept praying for this dear girl, and then for her new husband.

One day, while they were away on holiday, this couple got out of their car, knelt in a car park and without any human intervention, both accepted Christ as their own Saviour. When they came back to our church in Rockford, the husband gave a testimony during a Sunday morning service. He said, 'My wife and I owe our eternal salvation to the prayer-chains of this church.'

After they had gone away to study at a Bible college, the wife, as she related her experience to a group of staff wives, said, 'The thing that really astounded me after I came back home was that not one person of the one hundred and fifteen on those telephone prayer-chains gossiped. They all knew I had been married and divorced, and that this was my second husband, but no one else knew about it.'

That is the way it should be.

It's possible that some may find it difficult to keep juicy information confidential. If such is the case, they should call the leader and say, 'I would like my name removed from the prayer-chains.' This hasn't happened yet in our experience, but one day it might!

We have found that it is a great source of strength for prayer-chain members to sign the list of rules governing chain procedures at one time, while they are all together. In this way it is not a commitment to a person, or to a prayer-chain leader, but it is a commitment to God.

Our basic rules are few and simple. Members promise to pray *immediately* when receiving requests by telephone. They also promise to pass on the request immediately to the next person in the prayer-chain. They are not to delete anything or add anything to the request. And they are to keep it confidential – no gossiping.

The Strongest Link

Ordinary chains are as weak as their weakest link, but a prayer-chain is as strong as its strongest link. Why is this so? Because every single link in a prayer-chain, every member, is united from here on earth to God the Father in heaven. All, the weak and the strong, are praying simultaneously to God the Father, and we see the dramatic, exciting results here on earth.

In January 1968, we started with eight doubters, and in just a few months we had sixty-six pray-ers. From March to December, these sixty-six pray-ers prayed for 508 requests which multiplied to 33,528 prayers to God the Father, who sent back as many answers. Multiply your prayers on a chain and watch exciting things happen!

A chain reaction

Prayer-chains have a peculiar and wonderful way of linking people together. We found this out when our Jan made a long-distance telephone call from college to our prayer leader in Rockford — 325 miles away. The chain reaction started with her request on Tuesday, May 12, 1970: 'Pray for God to be with and help a lecturer [Jan's chemistry tutor] at Bethel, whose wife has a serious back problem. She was to have had immediate surgery, but they found out that she is pregnant. She has to be in bed much of the time and cannot take many pain pills as it might hurt the baby.' Periodically after that we prayed for Sharon.

Two years later, after moving from Rockford, I was having my first Bible study class in St Paul, when a young mother with a toddler in tow introduced herself to me in the church car park: 'I'm Sharon' she said.

'Are you *the* Sharon for whom our prayer-chains prayed when our Jan was so concerned about her chemistry tutor's wife?' I asked.

As she grinned and nodded, her girl-friend spoke up, 'Oh, Sharon, *that's why* you had such an easy delivery!'

Not long after that I was almost 2,000 miles away teaching the Six S's and telephone prayer-chains at a women's conference in California. I read some illustrations of prayer-chain requests directly from the bulging folder – my most powerful teaching tool! As I read the request Jan had 'phoned in from Bethel in 1970, a woman sitting in the back of the auditorium waved her hand to get my attention. She said, 'I have an urgent request from Sharon's mother-in-law. She just found out today that Sharon's husband's brother has an extremely serious brain tumor.' God gave to that roomful of women a tremendous sense of urgency as we broke into groups of four to practise and experience the reality of 'praying together.'

Returning to St. Paul, I immediately placed this pressing request with the staff wives' prayer-chain which we had recently started. Through the long, difficult illness and death of his brother, we continued to pray for this lecturer's need. And now, who do you think has been the telephone prayer leader of his staff wives' prayer-chain for the past two years? Yes, Sharon.

Sharon was also one of those chosen to be on my first personal prayer-chain in the Twin Cities. The chain is still active, and this last year the other members and I prayed for Sharon through another difficult pregnancy, through the baby's late arrival (timed to be after the brother's funeral), and the new baby's surgery. And we continued to pray about Sharon's back problem – for which we started prayer four and one-half years earlier in Rockford! In December 1974, Sharon had that surgery, and mother and baby are now doing beautifully.

Yes, telephone prayer-chains (as all forms of prayer) have a unique way of joining the human links together on a horizontal plane here on earth. But the marvel of it is that each individual is directly connected to the

source of power of the whole universe, who is in heaven
– God Himself!

'Lord, teach me to pray! Amen.'